The Leaning
Ivory Tower

Warren Bennis

with the assistance of
Patricia Ward Biederman

THE
LEANING
IVORY
TOWER

Jossey-Bass Publishers

San Francisco • Washington • London • 1973

THE LEANING IVORY TOWER
by Warren Bennis

Preface

The Leaning Ivory Tower is about universities in crisis, the crisis of agitation and disruption that roiled our campuses in the late sixties, culminating in the Kent State/Jackson State/Cambodia events of May 1970. It is about specific people and specific events and specific institutions and how lives and careers intersect with institutions and convulse during crisis. Crisis serves several positive purposes: It puffs up, ballonlike, the foibles and blemishes all our institutions contain but subdue or ignore during routine and stable times. Because options are reduced (or seem to be) during a crisis, the events enable people either to fulfill their potential and rise to the occasion or to collapse through withdrawing, under- or over-reacting, or hiding behind a dazed indifference. Most of all, crisis enables one to learn. There are no heroes or villains in most crises, just learners and nonlearners.

Part of what I learned during this period is recorded in *The Leaning Ivory Tower*—the personal part, as opposed to the possibly more objective, certainly less emotionally charged part. I felt a need, despite the problems, to write an "intimate memoir" that would capture the thoughts and feelings of a university administrator caught in the turmoil. I wanted to write a book from the inside out. Thus, the decision to write this book was easy, and an ideal arrangement presented itself. When I resigned from the State University of New York at Buffalo in August 1970, The Twentieth Century Fund agreed to aid in financing research for this work.

But the decision to publish wasn't easy. A number of questions, serious, fundamental questions, had to be answered before I could resolve my ambivalence. The questions were methodological, ethical, professional, and personal.

The methodological questions were the easiest to resolve (if not answer) because they were capable of intellectual resolution. These questions and my solution to them are in Chapter One. Essentially, the problem was the relationship and valdity of observed truth versus participative truth, an outsider's view versus an insider's view. Could I, writing as an actor integrally related to the action I was describing, broaden, if not transcend, the freedom of thought which our social institutions tend to confine and limit?

The ethical questions were and are much more difficult to resolve. How does one discuss individuals, friends, acquaintances, adversaries, without simplifying, vulgarizing, or caricaturing them? In Hamlet, Claudius suddenly comes alive when we see him praying. How to depict my friends, colleagues, adversaries in such a way as to enliven them, show them as full human beings, capture the nuance and subtlety of human interaction without cartoonlike description that flattens or trivializes or cheapens? How to record conversation and not have it sound like gossip? How to show everyone praying?

Another, possibly more consequential side of this problem is what my personal impressions might do to or for the individuals under discussion, myself included. I can rationalize: If the record and description and analysis in these pages are generally accurate and significant, if it is an account from which others can learn, if, from these pages, a modest and tender knowledge can be applied to similar situations, if the inevitably oversimplified descriptions of events and people avoid reckless character assaults, then the risks are warranted.

I am also concerned that the final chapters may give the

impression that Buffalo is no longer a viable institution. Buffalo is alive and well. Some of the former euphoria may be gone, but UB is healthy and continues to grow. Its faculty is strong, students are better every year; its excellences are many. The terrible space problems we encountered have eased somewhat, and the new campus we talked too much about has begun to rise in Amherst.

The personal and professional problems are interrelated, as indeed the preceding concerns are. As I read over the book, I realize that it is often too personal, displaying anguish, pride, and a strident honesty. And, as is almost always the case with intimate memoirs, it may hurt, offend, or fail to reach the people it would enlighten or convert. Some of what I wrote is ambivalent and gratuitous. There are pages of confession, expiation, apology, justification, and self-congratulation. And sometimes between the lines and sometimes frontally and stark there are details of personal achievement and even more of failure.

Do the survivors need the confession? Do I need expiation? If the wrong account were left to posterity, might some people be in harm's way? Is the book sufficiently important to risk giving uncertain answers? Should an account of this sort be published by someone now in a large, tax-supported institution? As a scholar, I would have no doubt about the answer to the last question. I don't believe in the censorship of ideas, even self-imposed censorship. But as a president, am I endangering the reputation of my institution by publishing this book?

After a long weekend with several of my erstwhile Buffalo colleagues and their wives (plus historian Walter Metzger as the "outside reader"), I realized that none of these questions could be answered completely or decisively, one way or another. I then asked two trusted and competent faculty members from the University of Cincinnati to critique the manuscript from an institutional point of view. The answer from both was clearcut: "If, for the sake of protecting the university or individuals mentioned in the book, the publication is postponed, the book's efficacy—not to speak of its topicality and hence the readers' interest—would be greatly reduced." Thus, the decision to publish. As I said, it wasn't easy. It was choosing the voice not of *I, Claudius* but, unmistakenly, of *De Profundis*.

The Leaning Ivory Tower can be easily summarized. It con-

cerns three universal organizational issues: succession and the search
for new leadership, dissent within large bureaucracies and several
ways it is suppressed and expressed, and the significant reform of
large-scale institutions. Chapters Two, Three, and Four deal with
succession; Chapter Five is on dissent; and the last two chapters
look at reform and give some guidelines for the administrator involved with reform.

As I glance over the written record, I recognize that my
ambivalence about publishing the book has not been fully resolved.
Some pages remind me of old-fashioned movie news features, with
the sepia-toned film and the overripe voices. Some pages still carry
the heavy weight of the Kent State days, when the campus air was
thick with acrid smoke. I don't believe I could write some of these
pages now. Not that the recorded scenes are necessarily wrong or
distorted, just slightly out of focus, the subtle lack of focus that
creates dissociation. But other passages show me the importance of
lessons learned in the past. These lessons deepen my ambivalence,
for now I see that the basic problem is how to apply them to the
present and future.

Claude and Nancy Welch, Saul and Linda Touster, Robert
and Karen O'Neil, Theodore and Elizabeth Friend, and Walter
Metzger spent a weekend in Cincinnati going over the manuscript
in detail and attempting to answer some of the questions raised in
this Preface. I wrote them a letter of thanks ending with the following paragraph: "Again, I want to thank all of you for making that
weekend one of the most important and fascinating and congenial
I have ever spent. If all goes right, Buffalo Lives. I hope the book
reflects the love and tension of it. Two cheers for the written word,
three cheers for love."

Guy Stern and Samuel Wilson of the University of Cincinnati read over the manuscript in its final form and attempted, at
my request, to examine its impact on our university since the president, as spokesman for the university (whether or not he inserts the
gratuitous disclaimer that he "speaks as an individual, not for the
university")', conceivably can cause damage to the university that a
private person or "mere" scholar cannot. Their sensitivity and sug-

gestions were extremely helpful in tipping the balance toward publication.

Nancy Clarkson read several of the most sensitive chapters in the first and second draft and made suggestions for which I will be forever grateful.

David Riesman was gracious enough, as he has always been since my graduate school days in Cambridge, to take time away from his sabbatical at the Institute for Advanced Studies to critique some of the early versions. His comments were consistently sharp and critical, often shaking me out of a reflexive bias, sometimes making me feel as if I were suddenly taken out of a comfortable hothouse and plunged into a large ice bucket.

Bruce Jackson was the only one, aside from my collaborator, Patricia Biederman, who read every chapter as it was extruded from my typewriter and then read the entire manuscript over and over again with increasing acuity and concern. He gave his time, wit, energy, and dazzling criticisms freely and generously, and I also shamelessly arrogated many of his notes and ideas.

William J. Miller, lifelong journalist and recently vice-president of public relations for Federated Department Stores, has worked with me over the past year, editing, restructuring, reanalyzing, excising, stitching, and adding enormously to whatever value and readability the book attained.

Finally, though she is listed on the title page as junior author, Patricia Biederman was not the ghost, but the incessant and invaluable Boswell, the person to whom this book owes most with the possible exception of my colleagues in the Buffalo Group —both those who remain and the expatriates—who will never be the same as a result of our formidable try.

Cincinnati   WARREN BENNIS
January 1973

Contents

The Leaning
Ivory Tower

To all those men and women—
in Buffalo, Cincinnati,
and on a thousand campuses great and small—
who strive with quiet courage
and unsung dedication
against apathy, anger, and often hopeless odds
to build a tower of learning
whose light can give meaning and purpose
to a world that grows more fragmented
the more it grows complex.
They are the allies of the future.

1

Personal Knowledge as Social Science: An Introduction

The elephant, says a Buddhist proverb, is the wisest of animals, the only one who remembers his former lives and who remains motionless for long periods of time meditating thereon. This book is the result of an elephantine year spent contemplating my former life as an administrator at the State University of New York at Buffalo. In it I have tried to reveal something of the inner workings of an American university of the early 1970s, an institution whose outer shell is familiar enough but whose daily administrative life has been clouded by a great informational void. A gentlemen's agreement protects the privacy of university administrators. Like most other bureaucrats they tend to be secretive about their work even when being secretive serves no obvious purpose, even when it is counterproductive. After working uncomfortably within the limits of this restrictive code for a number of years, I am convinced that it cries out for violation. One of the purposes of this book is to show why.

1

Too little has been written about the backstage life of *any* of the large bureaucratic institutions that dominate our "organized society." And stories by insiders are a rarity in the trickle of information that the public does receive. Like prisons, hospitals, ships, and the State Department, universities have a paranoid fear of betrayal. Mute loyalty is the favored emotion; according to this code, members can complain nonstop among themselves but never express their grievances in public.

One result of this institutional style is that the public's understanding of organizational life is often grossly inaccurate. The public sees only the product of organizational decision-making, never the process. Organizational behavior is typically perceived as monolithic. In fact, it rarely is. When the evening paper announces that the University of California or HEW or any other bureaucratic organization will pursue a particular course of action, the action is typically attributed to a composite body, the administration. This administration—whose parts vibrate in harmony and whose acts, because we are denied a look at the human drama that leads up to them, take on an air of superhuman detachment—is as mythical an animal as the griffin. Into every step taken by the "administration" goes a complicated pattern of meetings, disagreements, conversations, personalities, emotions, and missed connections like the ones described in this book. This very human process is bureaucratic politics. A parallel process is responsible for our foreign policy, the quality of our public schools, the scope and treatment of the news that the media choose to deliver to us each day. The public rarely sees the hundreds of small tableaux, the little dramas, that result in a policy statement or a bit of strategy. It sees only the move or hears only the statement, and it not unreasonably assumes that such an action is the result of a dispassionate, almost mechanical process in which problems are perceived, alternative solutions weighed, and rational decisions made. Given human nature, that is almost never the case.

This book is a fragmentary, impressionistic, very personal account of several critical events in the life of a university. In the pages that follow I record my firsthand experiences with three universal organizational phenomena—namely, leadership succession, resigning, and a new administration's attempt at massive organizational reform. I chose to limit my study to these three aspects of the administrative experience because each is rich with implications for many different bureaucratic settings. While the details may be idiosyncratic, the laws at work are the laws of bureaucracy in general, and the lessons to be learned apply to corporations and governments as well as universities.

Although I have tried to be objective, this is not journalism. It is an account of personal experiences from which I try to communicate to the general public some understanding about a peculiar and terribly important institution in our society, the university. The result is social science written from the inside; from the point of view of a reflective individual personally involved in the phenomena under analysis, often at the very center of the action. Thus, the book is simultaneously a dramatic account and a theoretical study of the university. Within this framework, the real-life actors and actual events become an integral part of the theoretical design and educational policy recommendations that are also included.

I must emphasize again the limits of my objectivity in writing this book. I approached the typewriter feeling a little like Saul Bellow's Herzog, buoyant with ideas and metaphysics and simultaneously weighed down by messy facts. I chose not to delete all my existential groanings. The Buffalo experience is still very close behind me, still too sensitively alive to present in a systematic, let alone truly objective, fashion. Instead of fighting the emotional content of the material, I have left it largely intact. The feelings are as much a part of the total experience as is the record of names and events. As a result, the emotional history of the Buffalo experience informs each page. Occasionally, instead of illuminating the situation, the emotion blocks the view, obscuring the larger, nonidiosyncratic picture. At those times I opt for specific truths over universal ones.

I found, as I wrote, that there is no suitable specialized vocabulary or appropriate theory to communicate the tentativeness, complexity, and ambiguity of the administrative phenomena I wanted to describe. At least, no such language or theory exists in the discipline I am most familiar with: organizational theory and the social sciences in general. This problem was most acute in discussing the exercise of power. I found myself looking for synonyms for "power" as if it were a five-letter obscenity. Norman Podhoretz's discussion in *Making It* of the distasteful aura around the word "ambition" is relevant here. In our culture the exercise of power is one of our "dirty little secrets." But even if one succeeds in avoiding the word, there is no way to avoid the concept. Power is what administrators wield. College administrators wield power in a limited but very real sense. How they choose to exercise power is one of the major themes of this book.

An even more persistent theme is the dichotomy in organizational life between theory and practice, the divergence of those who have knowledge but no power and those with power but no knowledge. This is a tragic, enormously frustrating, and virtually universal condition of life in organizations. All of my academic life and long before that, I have been intellectually preoccupied, virtually obsessed, with this dilemma, with the problem of *practical* intelligence, with the theory of practice, with the relationship between men who make history and the men who write it. My personal heroes are those individuals who embody and reconcile this dualism, individuals who have participated directly in the great events of their time—men like Malraux, Kennan, Clark Clifford, Frederick Taylor, Keynes, Brandeis, Harold Nicholson, and Camus, most of all Camus, who once scribbled in the margin of his diary what could be the personal slogan of all the others: "My greatest wish: to remain lucid in ecstasy." Knowing and working with Douglas McGregor when he was president and I a student at Antioch College furthered this fascination. As a result of McGregor's influence I decided to do graduate work at MIT under social psychologist Kurt Lewin, who said among many other things, "There is nothing so practical as a good theory," an aphorism I took to heart.

Preoccupation with the relationship of theory and practice is liable to bring on a permanent manic-depressive attitude toward the external events of one's experience. It is *always* the best of times and the worst of times. The theoretical breakthroughs arrive one on top of the other, and yet it is impossible to be sanguine in the face of the apparent impotence of social science research to affect fundamental matters: Vietnam policy, overpopulation, violence and crime, racial and intergroup conflict, the ecological trap. The numberless blue-ribbon task force reports, and the social science research upon which they are based, get better; but the problems get still worse. One sees remarkable, even great, men make terrible mistakes—not because they are ignorant or evil but because they seem incapable of acting on what they know. Some mysterious element seems to step in and disarm knowledge as a guide to action.

I regard this book as an initial contribution to an *exoteric* body of knowledge on the organizational life of universities. Esoteric knowledge is typically directed only toward experts. Exoteric means suitable to the general public; and it is precisely knowledge that can help in solving real-life problems that is most desperately needed in our major social organizations today.

This book deviates in two major respects from what is traditionally known as social science. The first involves a special methodology for dealing simultaneously with personal and "historical" material; the second has to do with the particular focus of the book. Both require some elaboration.

Method

Let me approach the issue of methodology indirectly by sharing two working titles that I considered but finally discarded. The first is from the opening stanza of Wallace Stevens' beautiful poem "The Man with the Blue Guitar." The whole stanza is so relevant I quote it in full:

> A man bent over his guitar,
> A shearsman of sorts. The day was green.
>
> They said, "You have a blue guitar,
> You do not play things as they are."
>
> The man replied, "Things as they are
> Are changed upon the blue guitar."
>
> And they said then, "But play, you must,
> A tune beyond us, yet ourselves,
>
> A tune upon the blue guitar
> Of things exactly as they are."[1]

[1] *The Collected Poems of Wallace Stevens* (New York: Knopf, 1955), pp. 165, 183.

Friends finally convinced me that *A Tune upon the Blue Guitar* was not the best title for a book on university administration, and yet it captures perfectly the book I intended. As Stevens writes in a later stanza:

Throw away the lights, the definitions,
and say of what you see in the dark.

That it is this or that it is that,
But do not use the rotted names.

How should you walk in that space and know
nothing of the madness of space,

Nothing of its jocular procreations?
Throw the lights away. Nothing must stand

Between you and the shapes you take
When the crust of shape has been destroyed.

You as you are? You are yourself.
The blue guitar surprises you.

Stevens' poem illustrates the particular bias I bring to this book, a belief that unnamed, untitled, and even unconceptualized experiences can be relearned in order to illuminate the darkness of human experience. Using the jargon of my trade, I suppose I could say that I wanted to write a book about the "phenomenology of power." Stevens says it far less pretentiously with "A tune upon the blue guitar/Of things exactly as they are."

In writing, I wanted to reestablish *reflection* as a legitimate process of inquiry for the social sciences. I needed a "roll-your-own" methodology, which would integrate raw experience with analysis. This approach grows out of what I see as a new role for the social scientist, a role that combines action and analysis. In this role, the scientist is more akin to the "new journalist," with his personal voice and cold impersonal eye, than to most of the current writers in social science. Instead of the more traditional "participant-observer" familiar to the anthropologist, the field sociologist, and the psychologist, the social scientist in this mode becomes an "observant participant." This approach allows for both personal and theoretical insights. Both are in gear, but one, the personal, is the major stem-winder.

It is ironic but inevitable that a social scientist trained during the tight-lipped fifties should be concerned with finding an alternative, experiential approach to organizational analysis. In that decade, as well as the two surrounding it, logical positivism dominated most of social science education. Some of us were bound to look for a corrective to the nonemotional, "objective" approach our teachers emphasized.

This leads me to the second title I considered for the book, W. H. Auden's line, "Thou shalt not/Commit a social science." Auden's words are instructive. Most social science writing about men in institutions suffers from a sanitary concern with causality, coherence, and a search for pattern which rarely exists except in the mind of the observer. The result is false, at times destructively so. Those elements of confusion, chance, ignorance, stupidity, reckless-ness, as well as the many amiable qualities of man, are simply not reckoned with; they are selectively ignored.

In an article on the role of "historian as eye-witness," Arthur Schlesinger has discussed similar methodological matters with great precision and style. In the course of the discussion, Schlesinger cites Lionel Trilling's essay on Tacitus, in which Trilling challenges the value of "objectivity" in the social sciences, with special reference to history: "To minds of a certain sensitivity 'the long view' is the falsest historical view of all, and indeed the insistence on the length of perspective is intended precisely to overcome sensitivity. Seen from sufficient distance, it says, the corpses and the hacked limbs are not so terrible, and eventually they even begin to compose themselves into a 'meaningful' pattern."[2]

Most conventional social science writing presents two extreme caricatures of organizational life. One is the result of "dust-bowl" empiricism, the census-survey approach, which accounts for every moving thing except real life and growth. The second is a function of an exaggerated reliance on the general theoretical statement, preferably in mathematical form. The problem with statistics and

---

[2] "The Historian as Participant," *Daedalus*, 1971, *100*.

formulas is that, by themselves and without nuance, they have little meaning. Uninterpreted body counts and voting patterns, accurate though they may be, are not terribly relevant to the real-life organization.

The lifelessness of most social science written today is made embarrassingly obvious in light of the work being done in traditional social science areas by the "new journalists," that formidably talented generation of nonscientists. The new journalism is fascinated with the important human activities of our time, particularly those that take place in an organizational setting. New journalists have taken as subject matter cultural phenomena as divergent as newspaper empires, a king of the pimps, the Mafia, the drug scene, moon shots, the *New Yorker,* and "radical chic" cocktail parties. Mainstream social science never looked more pallid than when compared with the pop social analysis of such writers as Tom Wolfe, Truman Capote, Norman Mailer, Gay Talese, and Gail Sheehy, who have not been afraid to venture into the difficult territory of personal *feeling* in order to provide a truer picture of events. This, in itself, is good; the rub is that the new journalists, shrewd observers and exciting writers, often lack a conceptual bite. Good journalism is often very bad social science. And yet social scientists have, by default, turned large areas of contemporary experience over to amateurs.

Tepid prose style is not the heart of the matter, but only the superficial consequence of an underlying reticence that has necessarily constrained most contemporary social science. By standing aloof from the action and by guarding against personal feelings, the social scientist not only denies his own integrity; he often loses sight of the larger reality beyond the immediate crisis or the conceptual apparatus. Schlesinger again provides an apt quotation, this time from Emerson: "Time dissipates to shining ether the solid angularity of facts." Like the proverbial reporter standing at the elbow of history taking down middle initials, the disengaged social scientist may find himself with a notebook full of inconsequential "facts." As a result, the general reading public must continue to rely on the picture of human institutions obtained in the popular press. Depending on its sophistication, that means either new journalism, which often indulges in liberal stereotyping, or the simplistic

Reader's Digest version, in which any American bureaucratic organization usually emerges as a hallowed shrine. Both views are limited.

It is appropriate that social science step in to fill the informational void that has been partially but inadequately met by journalistic social analysis. The public desperately needs rigorous scientific study of contemporary social phenomena. Consider the recent example of the press's analysis of the Pentagon papers. In trying to understand the Ellsberg case, the public had to rely exclusively on the media. Yet most newspaper accounts reduced the Pentagon bureaucracy to a collection of fools or knaves, trapped in a cat's cradle of red tape, caught in deceit and counterdeceit; then, like tenderfoot scouts, bungling the job of covering up their footprints. A more scientific treatment of the incident would see the Pentagon officials as victimized to a large extent by the same bureaucracy in which 90 per cent of the working class of this country gains its sustenance, the bureaucracy it lives with, and curses at, practically every day of its working life. But reading Tom Wicker and James Reston of the *Times*, one gets the impression that the Pentagon invented and perfected bureaucratic bungling—as if the *Times* itself were not held by the same heavy hand. These "revelations" are no better than the obverse glorification we see on the front pages most other days of the week. Both approaches represent a denial of the frail humanness of institutions.

In describing troubled campuses, this book attempts to avoid these extremes without falling into middle-of-the-roadism. Its point of view is out of the corner of the eye, where one can never completely focus during the period of action and one is fully aware of the import of events only when the action ebbs. I try to enter, as do the new journalists, difficult and personal territories of feeling, in the hope of staking out an area that future social scientists will develop more fully. I use the language of myth rather than the language of science in borrowing from Kenneth Burke his critical device, the "representative anecdote"; that is, a singular event with antecedents and consequences capable of consolidating illuminations that hold true not only for the described event but for the entire class of cases for which the anecdote stands. I record as far as possible every homely, quotidian detail in the belief that to look closely is to be surprised. The impulse behind this method is expressed in a bit of dialogue from Malraux. "How," one of his characters asks, "can one make the best use of one's life?" "By converting as wide a range of experience as possible into conscious thought."

The result of this approach—"methodology" is too grand a word—is not untrammeled subjectivity. I tried to keep always in mind a number of questions which served as guides, as *controls* over my subjectivity. For example, I tested all of the material against the following questions: Are my interpretations, analyses, and policy recommendations consistent with the facts and theory? Are the findings and conclusions consistent with those found in other social settings? Do I manifest a lack of distortion in reporting and sufficient distance from other actors? Does the material (especially the conclusions) have plausibility?

Inherent to the very process of studying human phenomena— especially when the researcher is himself one of the actors under study—is a built-in distortion, usually referred to as the "reflexive dilemma." Physicists can disassociate themselves from the atom; biologists can distinguish themselves from the cell. But how can a social scientist acquire the necessary detachment to claim objectivity? As Freud once joked, the only trouble with self-analysis is countertransference. I know of no answer to this problem beyond acknowledging it and hoping that it may prove a corrective to another, more critical dilemma, given classic expression by de Tocqueville.

> I have come across men of letters, who have written history without taking part in public affairs, and politicians, who have only concerned themselves with producing events without thinking of describing them. I have observed that the first are always inclined to find general causes where the others, living in the midst of disconnected daily facts, are prone to imagine that everything is attributable to particular incidents, and that the wires they pull are the same that move the world. It is to be presumed that they both are equally deceived.

These problems are not to be taken lightly. Both types of distortions undoubtedly played a role in this book, though not so great a role, I hope, as to lessen its credibility. Having tried the engaged approach, I am convinced that "participative truth" is simply different from observed truth. Each should be capable of informing the other.

Focus

In 1970 alone, well over twelve hundred books were published on the subject of education. That is a significant jump over the six hundred or so published annually during the 1960s. A large number of these books dissected, analyzed, categorized, and conceptualized the college disruptions which burst on the American scene in force following the Berkeley Free Speech riots of 1964–65. The other books focused on problems of access and equal opportunity, teaching and learning, innovation, and assorted other topics. Many of these were excellent, especially those written by individuals who were not "educationists." But I can think of only a handful of books that have treated the university as a social system, as an organization, as a highly complex and interacting system of people and groups. The paucity of work in this area may be related to the reflexive dilemma mentioned above. University researchers study everything from taxi dancers to the number seven (plus or minus two), but they have largely left unexamined their own institution, its tribal customs and patterns.

I first proposed a highly personal study of the organizational dynamics of a university shortly after becoming provost at Buffalo in September 1967. At that time I wrote to the president of a social science research foundation, requesting a small grant to employ a young, postdoctoral fellow to act as "social diarist" for my administration. It was my hope to detail the administrative experiences of at least a year by compiling daily interviews, recording all my interactions, comparing my institutional goals with progress made toward them, and collecting observations and questionnaires. The outcome was to be, in the prose of the grant application, "a small book that would describe in detail the administrative-leadership processes in a large-scale public university, a book that would relate my own theories of organizational behavior (as well as others') to my own recent experience, with the hope of contributing increased understanding of the social architecture of higher education, appropriate for the twentieth century."

The project evoked some interest but was abandoned when I discovered the scarcity of social diarists. In lieu of a systematic collaboration, I settled for a personal diary, an erratic journal of events in which I participated. The results were alarming. After only a month or so, I reluctantly decided that written organizational theories, even those I had devised myself, had very little relationship to what I was actually doing. Indeed, where theory and practice touched, they were barely tangent. More often they were at embarrassing cross-purposes. Once again I changed the format of the exercise and decided to keep a double-entry book, not with financial debts and credits but with theory on one side and practice on the other. Each new day strengthened a growing conviction that theory unproved in practice is majestically useless. One of the results of that double-entry ledger is this book.

The university that emerges in the following pages is a large, richly endowed, and socially crucial bureaucracy. I am aware that the word "bureaucracy" has negative connotations in our society, that it suggests some combination of faceless robot and fierce behemoth. But I use the term more or less neutrally to identify a kind of social system that has dominated all industrial societies; that, indeed, pervades most Marxist societies as well as democratic ones. Hospitals, research and consulting organizations, the media, industry, welfare organizations, the universities—they are all bureaucratized social systems.

In order to understand the complex workings of any of these bureaucratic organizations, it helps to see them in action, changing, in motion. The period of the book was a uniquely unsettled time in the history of higher education. However difficult campus crisis is to live with as a captive participant, it is a splendid instrument for observation. A crisis jolts and unfreezes the system, upsets expectations, and tests received truths. It also reveals any underlying fissures so easy to ignore during times of stability and calm. For an administrator in a university over the past few years, crises came in pairs and trios. They provided, among other things, an unsettling vehicle for arriving at a more thorough understanding of the organization than the previous fifteen years of relatively low turbulence ever provided.

The one bias that pervades my analysis of the university,

and my own work as a university president, is a conviction that any campus bureaucracy—indeed, any bureaucracy—to be successful must establish a "truth-in-administration" policy. All our American institutions are facing an increasing credibility gap and are under pressure to communicate more honestly with their publics, more openly, more simply, and more humanely. This demand for candor is good, though occasionally painful. It forces the university, the company, the government to define its goals precisely and makes it harder to hide behind self-serving and defensive evasions and euphemisms.

There are times, of course, when total candor is not possible or even wise. In our competitive society, secrecy may sometimes be the greater virtue. But bureaucracies have senselessly indulged in secrecy for its own sake to such an extent that they have lost public trust. As I write this, 47 per cent of the American people, according to polls, believe that "a real breakdown in this country" is pending; 71 per cent to 85 per cent believe that the "real story" from Washington seldom makes its way into the news, and over half of the ghetto population of Washington, D.C., doubts that Neil Armstrong ever walked on the moon, believing instead that the walk was staged in a studio somewhere by the government.

An administrative style of evasions, lies, and euphemisms is not conducive to what the late historian Richard Hofstadter called "socially responsible criticism." Instead, an "adversary culture" develops, as it has so noisily in America over the last few years. If those of us who lead institutions could be more honest and forthcoming, straighter and more direct, more willing to admit errors, a socially responsible, critical audience might reasonably be expected to emerge.

Besides destroying credibility, lack of candor has a devastating impact on the *effectiveness and morality* of our institutions. As Tom Wicker commented in a speech at Harvard:

> This old war, from beginning to end, has been rooted in misapprehension. I recall being in Vietnam in early '66 with Hubert Humphrey, who was then Vice President. At the conclusion of that trip we were taken around to the Ambassador's house. The Ambassador was Henry Cabot Lodge. . . . Mr. Lodge sat at one side of the portico there, and the Vice President of the

United States sat at the other side, and they lined up the television
cameras back here and in between sat six hapless, helpless American advisors to local district officials, and they said, "Fellas, how's
it going?" They told him how it was going. It was going pretty
good. And I was a rookie at that game and was taking notes pretty
madly there, and a friend of mine who had spent two years in
Vietnam came up to me and said, "This sounds pretty good,
doesn't it? You ought to have heard what that fellow told me the
other night when I was talking with him in his tent. What he said
did not go anywhere near what he said on the television cameras."[3]

This is not uncommon, as we all know. Wicker himself tells
of more serious deceits with respect to the Vietnam war. What is
even more frightening is the frequent lack of candor *within* large
organizations. In his book *The Twilight of the Presidency*, George
Reedy, who was press secretary to President Johnson, argues that
bodyguards, protocol, and a staff eager to tell him what he wants
to hear prevent any President from keeping in touch with reality.
In *Man of Destiny*, George Bernard Shaw's Napoleon is constantly
frustrated by the bumbling actions of a young lieutenant. In despera-
tion, Napoleon asks an innkeeper, "Guiseppe, what will we do with
this lieutenant? Everything he says is all wrong." The innkeeper
answers, "Make him a general. Then everything he says will be
all right." It is no wonder that organizations fail when decision-
making is based on feedback from yes-men.

The case of the Pentagon papers is only one recent demon-
stration of the chronic inability of large-scale bureaucracies to come
clean with the public, of their chronic failure to trust people, which
after all is the ultimate basis of the democratic system. There is
little hope that this situation will improve until the internal life of
these organizations changes. No organization can be honest with the
public if it is not honest or straight *within,* any more than an individual can be honest with another unless he is in valid communication with himself.

The future of the university depends heavily on the viability
of all our human institutions. These institutions must develop the
capacity to adapt, to make intelligent reforms, to be open to new

---

[3] "Notes and Comment," *The New Yorker,* March 6, 1971, pp. 27–29.

data, to see reality. They are absolutely imperative *musts* if our institutions are to be vital, effective, and humane. If not, we can expect only a greatly diminished future, very like that described in Yevtushenko's chilling triplet:

> One day posterity will remember
> This strange era, these strange times,
> When honesty was called courage.[4]

[4] "Conversation with an American Writer," from Vladimir Markov and Merrill Sparks (Eds. and Trans.), *Modern Russian Poetry* (London: MacGibbon and Klee, 1966), p. 777. My reading.

2

Searching for the "Perfect" President

~~~~~~~~~~~~~~~~~~~~~~~~~~~~~~~~~~~~~

"**D**id you see the Meyerson announcement? It's awful, just awful." Seymour Knox was lamenting Martin Meyerson's decision, announced in January 1970, to step down from the presidency of State University of New York at Buffalo in order to succeed Gaylord Harnwell as president of the University of Pennsylvania. As chairman of the Buffalo council, Knox had been crucial in bringing Meyerson to Buffalo over the cries of a local faction determined to block the appointment of "that Jew from Berkeley." Therefore, Knox was not happy about Meyerson's decision to move on.

"I feel like a crumb-bum," he complained. "Yesterday, in Philadelphia, I ran into an old friend, Bill Day, who is now chairman of the Penn Board of Trustees. Was he gloating! God, it was awful. I felt like he'd stolen my cook."

Adapted from my article in the April 1971 issue of *Atlantic Monthly*.

16

The stolen cook was not the first analogy to come to my mind, but I knew what Knox meant. University presidents are currently somewhat harder to find and keep than competent domestic help. The numbers fluctuate, but a sizable list of colleges and universities are currently conducting presidential searches. Why are there so many openings at the top? There are many reasons, but a root cause is the altered nature of the job itself. There was a time when a university president did little more than officiate at commencements and raise funds; when his tenure was roughly equal to that of a Supreme Court Justice. Not today. In the aftermath of Berkeley, Columbia, Harvard, and Kent State, a university president is a full-time crisis manager. He remains in office less than five years on the average, and is usually glad to retire. Annual turnover of university and college presidents has jumped nearly 30 per cent in the last three years. In the first two months of 1970, new presidents were named at forty-two colleges, while one hundred resigned during the first six months of 1970. One analyst has compared the job unfavorably with that of a pro hockey referee. I don't think he's far off the mark. The work is rough, physically exhausting, even dangerous. University presidents may lose fewer teeth than hockey officials, but they have a startling number of heart attacks. A modern university president is expected to have practical vision, a good track record in administration, and national prominence as a scholar. He must be a good public speaker, fundraiser, writer, analyst, friend and colleague, manipulator of power, planner, coworker, persuader, and disciplinarian. He must have an attractive family and an indefatigable and effortlessly sociable wife. He must be a Money Man, Academic Manager, Father Figure, Public Relations Man, Political Man, and Educator. In short, as one Harvard man put it, looking toward Nathan Pusey's successor, "He must be a messiah with a good speaking voice." Or as Herman B. Wells, former president of Indiana University, said in a rather more earthy way: "He should be born with the physical strength of a Greek athlete, the cunning of a Machiavelli, the wisdom of a Solomon, the courage of a lion, if possible. But in any case he must be born with the stomach of a goat."

During the last several years, while serving in various administrative posts at State University of New York at Buffalo, I was considered for the presidencies of at least a dozen colleges and universities. Since scrutiny works both ways, the time I spent with search committees (being examined rather like a bolt of felt, as I sometimes thought) gave me an excellent opportunity to study the process by which our universities choose presidents. Each of the twelve or so searches in which I was a participant-observer was unique. However, one search in particular—Northwestern University's—illustrates better than fiction the clash of formal machinery and partisan pressures in which American university presidents are made.

In simpler, less turbulent times, the presidential search process was handled much the way an exclusive men's club chooses a new member. John G. Bowman, chancellor of the University of Pittsburgh in the twenties, recalls his own selection by this method:

> On an afternoon in October 1920, in my work as the Director of the American College of Surgeons, I made a talk in Pittsburgh. The room was full of people, most of them interested in hospitals and the practice of medicine. After the talk, two or three men asked me to have dinner with them and some others that evening at the Duquesne Club. I said yes.
>
> In the evening I met about a score of men, most of them strangers to me, gathered around a table in a private dining room. During the dinner and after the dinner they asked questions: Do university presidents have business sense? What in your opinion is the top value of a college education? Is a college education a good thing for everybody? On and on the questions went. We had a lively talk and a good time. At about ten o'clock, one of the men at the table asked me to step into the hall with him. We went out of the room and walked down the hall toward a window hung with heavy draperies.
>
> We had covered only half the distance to the window, however, when another man of the group opened the door and asked us to come back. Then, all at the table again, George H. Clapp, head of Pittsburgh Testing Laboratories, said to me, "These men are trustees of the University of Pittsburgh. For some weeks we have been gathering information about you. We are glad now to invite you to become Chancellor of the University."[1]

Bowman's story has a nostalgic quaintness to it, like a Dreiser novel, but the process he describes was not at all unusual. Douglas

---

[1] *Unofficial Notes by John G. Bowman* (Pittsburgh, 1963), pp. 4–5.

McGregor, president of Antioch College from 1948 to 1954, once told me about his selection. He was in his office, at MIT, when his secretary told him that a Mr. Arthur Morgan was waiting to see him. McGregor knew little of Antioch and nothing of Morgan, who had been president of the college. Morgan offered him the presidency of Antioch after a few minutes of polite conversation, which ran the gamut from the weather to the Charles River snaking below the window of McGregor's office. They talked a while longer, and the next afternoon the two of them took the train from the Back Bay Station for Yellow Springs, Ohio.

Even in the old days, naming one's successor was rather unusual (although after David Jordan left Indiana University to become president of Stanford, the Indiana board asked him to name not only his immediate successor but the next three presidents as well). The selection of a new president was most often the once-in-a-lifetime task of the board of trustees or the university corporation. Board members usually knew a few well-placed individuals to call on to suggest nominees, and people like Andrew S. White, the first president of Cornell University, Nicholas Murray Butler, or Chancellor William Tolley of Syracuse were frequently consulted. White, for example, personally picked two presidents for Michigan, one for Indiana, one for California, and one for Brown; he also suggested the men who became the first presidents of Stanford and Johns Hopkins. In the 1920s, few boards reached their final decision without having consulted the Rockefeller Foundation. More recently, the Ford and Carnegie Foundations have played crucial roles in identifying potential presidents.

But times have changed. Today, universities are expected to choose presidents in the open by a process involving students and faculty in some meaningful way. The process is expected to be a democratic one—although, in my experience, it falls considerably short of that ideal.

Take Northwestern. Mid-November 1969, my office at Buffalo received a call from the Chicago office of the management consulting firm of Booz, Allen, and Hamilton. I didn't return the call immediately. (I had mistakenly assumed that Booz, Allen, and Hamilton was going to ask me to give a speech on management—a practice I had discontinued because I felt increasingly

squeamish lecturing on problems I had written books about now
that my own institution was suffering with the symptoms I was
reputedly an expert in curing. I recalled Auden's character "who
lectured on navigation while the ship was going down.")

Two days before Thanksgiving, I learned that the firm was
acting as consultant for Northwestern University. Their man wanted
to know if I might be available for, "or at least interested enough
to explore," the Northwestern presidency. "I'm not really sure," I
answered. "I don't know a great deal about Northwestern and what
it wants. But I would like to discuss it with you." He asked me when
I could come out to Chicago or make time available for him at
Buffalo. I told him that it would be very tough to find any free
time before mid-January, but that I would be in Cleveland over the
Thanksgiving weekend, and if he could manage to come there, I
could certainly see him on Friday or Saturday. He said that a man
in their Cleveland office "who has been working on the Northwestern case" would be able to see me at my in-laws' home in
Cleveland.

I cannot recall Booz, Allen's Cleveland man by name. He
reminded me of many youngish management consultants I have
known. He was a Harvard Business School graduate, WASPish,
attractive, crisp, alert, and formidably informed. We spent about
three hours together and hit it off immediately. I felt he was as
straightforward and honest as he could be about the Northwestern
situation. He gave me an exhaustive survey of the present status and
future of Northwestern, told me a little about the search activities
to date, indicated generally what kind of man they were looking for
and how Booz, Allen came to be involved in "coordinating the
search process," and gave an informal rundown of some of the
people on the board of trustees. At the end of the discussion, I presented my *curriculum vitae*. He told me that I would be hearing
from them in the future.

What I learned at that time was this. Northwestern sounded
first-rate. It had a healthy endowment, distinguished faculty, top-
caliber students, and rich and prominent trustees. Moreover, it was
untainted, so far, by "the troubles" its more distinguished neighbor,
the University of Chicago, had experienced during the past three
years or so. Undertaking the presidential search was an omnibus

committee consisting of nine trustees, four faculty members (elected by the faculty), and three students. Booz, Allen had collected the names of more than three hundred possible candidates from the faculty, the board of trustees, and students. The incumbent president, a former dean of the Northwestern medical school, Rocky Miller, was close to sixty-eight years old, mandatory retirement age, and had been in office for about twenty years. He had been, according to my informant, a good, somewhat conservative president who was instrumental in bringing about a substantial building program at Northwestern. With Booz, Allen's help, the search committee had drawn up a three-page document describing the kind of man they were looking for to replace Miller. Dr. Right was married, between thirty-five and forty years of age, with a strong, broad academic background, administrative experience, vision, energy, good health, and an ability to talk with diverse constituencies, and someone who could keep the campus relatively free from disruption. Booz, Allen was in the act because the board felt that a good consulting firm, with a strong track record for executive "headhunting," could assist in the normally chaotic selection process. I also learned that Jim Allen, a Northwestern trustee, was the "Allen" in Booz, Allen & Hamilton.[2]

I was very taken with Northwestern after that talk and felt highly complimented by their interest in me. Several factors contributed to my initial enthusiasm: Northwestern was in an important urban area which the university had virtually ignored in the past and with which it now wanted to get involved. The university had yet to achieve "greatness" in the same sense that Harvard or Yale or even Stanford had (Stanford most of all, since twenty years ago Stanford was in about the same league as Northwestern) despite its valid claim to top-rank faculty and students. There was not yet a truly unique character associated with Northwestern, no Northwesternness, but the search committee obviously wanted such a character to emerge under new leadership. All of these suggested to me that Northwestern was on the verge of major

---

[2] Booz, Allen had actually created the presidential vacancy, it seems. It was Booz, Allen that recommended that Miller be moved up from president to chancellor as part of an administrative reorganization plan commissioned earlier by the Northwestern board.

growth and that its new president would play a key role in directing
its emergence as a major university.

Whatever doubts I had centered on whether Northwestern
and I fit. From all I knew of Northwestern, it was conservative, rich,
suburban, and Midwestern—what in the 1950s would have been
called a "white shoe" campus. The trustees were the biggest question in my mind. For the most part they came from the large banks,
law firms, and businesses in Chicago. They not only read the *Chicago Tribune* editorials daily, but, according to my Booz, Allen &
Hamilton man, they actually *believed* them. Boards have an understandable tendency to pick presidents who incline to agree with their
values if not their politics. (One study of 110 state college and university presidents showed that 88 per cent had the same political
affiliation as the governors of their respective states.) Whether or
not they would find me acceptable remained to be seen. That a consulting firm had been called in—no matter one of the best—also
registered a blip of concern. Previous experience with presidential
searches led me to believe that this was extremely atypical. So I had
a few qualms, and I knew there would be surprises ahead. But even
when one is prepared for surprises, they do surprise all the same.

A week or so later, my first caller from Booz, Allen called.
Without really using these words, he told me that I had passed the
first hurdle and would hear from him again in a month or so. Apparently, there were other people to screen, and if I stood up well,
a contingent from Northwestern would visit me in Buffalo. He was
extremely friendly, even solicitous. "Do you want any more information about Northwestern?" he asked before ringing off.

Sometime in the first half of January 1970, I was called
again. The search was going along nicely, my Booz, Allen contact
reported. The list was now pared down to fifteen or twenty names.
He said that I was still very much in the running; indeed, he
wondered whether I could meet with the chairman of the search
committee, who was also a Northwestern trustee and chairman of
the board of Harris Trust Company in Chicago; the associate dean
of Northwestern's school of speech and drama, representing the
faculty; and the president of the Northwestern student association.
We set the time for February 4 in my office at Buffalo.

The group arrived there around 10 o'clock in the morning

and left for the airport at 4 in the afternoon. Lunch was brought in. It was a six-hour talk show. After the initial awkwardness was smoothed over with orders for coffee or tea and talk of their flight, we settled down for some serious conversation. We covered a range of topics: campus unrest, my role at Buffalo, my attitudes about student participation, all the way to social activities and family. (They did not ask whether I had a "Hebrew strain," as one trustee of Penn State had the year before, when he visited me at Buffalo. At that time I replied that the quality of my Hebrewness was not strained; I was, indeed, a "Hebrew." "I knew it! I knew it!" the trustee exclaimed enthusiastically.)

The time with the three search committee members was well spent. We covered a lot of ground, and it was clear that they not only permitted but encouraged me to indicate how I stand and who I am. They had read some of my books and articles and referred several times to a revealing interview with me which had appeared in the February 1969 *Psychology Today*.

In any case, all of us seemed to enjoy the day. The faculty member wanted to know whether I cared more about academic pursuits than administrative affairs and whether I would work with, rather than against, the faculty. Faculty tend to view or want to view the president as their servant, not their seer, he said. The student clearly wanted a president who would take the students into account, not just in a token way, and he dwelt on problems of student involvement in the political processes of the university. The chairman and I got into a little argument concerning the tenure of presidents. I said rather firmly that I believed in a term appointment of about seven years, as Kingman Brewster had recently advocated at Yale, rather than a lifelong appointment. This caused the chairman to ask whether I was really interested in Northwestern and whether it might not be "a mistake to set a definite period of office." The discussion was easy, flowing, informal, and without a great deal of anxiety.

The sticky points were all predictable. I asked them a battery of questions about Northwestern's culture and style, its financial status and outlook, its relationship with other universities in the area and with the cities and state. I also asked about the number of "disadvantaged" students admitted; about black studies programs in general; and about presidential discretion and power, the structure of the search committee, the weaknesses in the present organization of the university, an evaluation of the present administration, relations with alumni, and so on.

I *liked* them, particularly the student, who asked the most penetrating and direct questions. The faculty representative appeared to be gentle and perceptive and a remarkable listener. The chairman was the least relaxed and sometimes irrelevant, going off on a tack of his own which I couldn't always understand. He was clearly concerned about campus disorders, but he appeared to be a broad-minded and open man.

When the three returned to Northwestern, they met with Booz, Allen for a two- or three-hour "debriefing." On the basis of their reports, Booz, Allen prepared a summary of their impressions:

SUMMARY COMMENTS FROM
SUBCOMMITTEE MEETING WITH
PROSPECTIVE CANDIDATE

WARREN G. BENNIS
Acting Executive Vice President
and Vice President-Academic Development
State University of New York at Buffalo
Buffalo, New York

ACADEMIC QUALIFICATIONS AND EXPERIENCE

Strong qualifications and credentials. Full professor—two institutions. Innovative and progressive. Some national eminence through extensive writing and lecturing. Favorably inclined to professional fields as well as academic —"cultural pluralism." Both a teacher and writer. Evidently strong faculty/student relations and sensitivity. Former President Meyerson's selection of him is tribute to his academic as well as administrative credentials. Buffalo and state university affiliation should not be held against him. The university has made many significant changes and improvements.

A dissenting opinion by one subcommittee member—"compulsive speaker and writer— perhaps has overdone it."

EXECUTIVE EXPERIENCE	Has handled key issues of the "number-two" job at Buffalo very well under heavy pressure. Clear understanding of how the administrative structure can complement, even aid, the development of new progressive currents in the field of higher education. Has played key role in the improvements made at Buffalo. Is an innovative administrator—many new programs evidently well planned and executed. Delegates well. Personally well organized; firmminded; appears to be decisive and no impressions of limitations in leadership. Consensus opinion that he can contribute, but we must check his track record—Is he a senior *executive* or merely an able, persuasive administrator?
MAGNITUDE OF PRESENT MANAGEMENT RESPONSIBILITY	Experience is applicable but effectiveness has not been proven over extended period. Chief operating officer for past several months of sizable, complex, urban, public university. Larger in enrollment than Northwestern but not as broad in scope. Helped effect necessary and important changes from private to public institution management. Important to recall that he had significant experience as a professor and department chairman at a large, private university (MIT). Is not tied to any system of organization and expressed reservations on Buffalo multiarea provost system. Also raised questions on NU organization, but appears to be objective and open-minded. Works hard at managing and evidently is very demanding.
PERSONAL QUALIFICATIONS	Medium height, "tweedy," "modernish" but neat. Personal bearing "taller than his physical stature." Poised, articulate, charming, genuine, and businesslike warmth. A quality man. Smart, analytical—once he makes decisions will be demanding and perhaps unbending. Could work well at all levels. Will want authority but suspect he would be sensitive to others. Community-minded and gives impression that his wife is equally extroverted (al-

though subcommittee did not meet her).
While affable and thoughtful, there is clear
indication of firm-mindedness and high opinion of self. [A possible, but not serious, reserva-
tion that his manner might not "sit well" with
some faculty, trustees, and alumni.]

APPARENT
INTEREST IN
THE POSITION

Very high. Really "did his homework" on NU.
Asked extremely good questions. Sees Northwestern as logical and attractive next step for
him. Sees the university as an academic institution of great accomplishment and potential.
[Would want to come only if he were convinced he could ultimately become the chief
executive.] Was sensitive to the importance of
the relationship with the chancellor—raised
subject himself.

SUMMARY
COMMENTS

A good meeting. Personally and professionally
attractive. Handled himself well. Has a style
that might be just right for the coming era at
Northwestern. An impressive, innovative, competent, and accomplished administrator. May
be limited in experience and a bit too aggressive and demanding, but is a strong candidate
who should be considered further.

Similar profiles were drawn up on twenty of the stronger
candidates and distributed among the search committee. (The
profiles were kept, along with other search materials, in elegant
black notebooks, each embossed in gold with the member's name.)

Two weeks after my interview, the Booz, Allen representative phoned again with positive joy in his voice. The search committee wanted me to come to Northwestern to spend at least a day
or two talking with people. He was annoyed that two key Northwestern faculty committees had "demanded" the right to interview
all "serious" candidates, and he hoped I wouldn't mind if they were
included in my visit. "The more the better," I said, and we settled
on March 7 for my visit.

On March 7, the Buffalo campus exploded into one of the
worst crises to hit major campuses in America. Strangely enough,
except for then faculty member Edgar Z. Friedenberg's articles in
the *New York Review of Books,* a squib in *Newsweek,* and an occa-

sional story in the *New York Times,* the *Post,* and the *National Observer,* there was little national coverage of the Buffalo crisis. Perhaps people were getting bored or inured to the guerrilla activities of students and the police (this was *before* Kent State and Jackson State), or maybe the Santa Barbara bank burning about the same time eclipsed everything else. In any case, the Buffalo campus experienced an unparalleled convulsion, with the local press reporting fresh disasters daily. In the course of several months of disruption at Buffalo, more than 125 students, police, and others required medical attention. Forty-five faculty members were arrested and booked on three separate charges (the largest number of faculty ever arrested for a campus protest activity; the previous record was sixteen Harvard faculty arrested for protesting the Spanish-American War). Another six faculty members were arrested on other counts. More than fifty students were charged on criminal counts. Over three hundred thousand dollars in property damage was reported.

At seven that morning, March 7, on the plane for Chicago, I wasn't at all certain that I should be going. I had averaged only two hours sleep per night over the past three weeks. (If there is any advice I would give campus administrators during a crisis, it is this: *get sleep.* The kids are younger and there are more of them. They can run in relays.) I felt like limp pasta as I flopped into my seat. I was no more up to what I knew would be a grueling day of scrutiny than I was to another day of manning the barricades on my own campus.

Worse by far than the fatigue was the recognition that I *should* remain in Buffalo that day in order to stave off a decision made by certain members of the university's administration the night before. Buffalo's acting president, Peter Regan, and some of his advisors were convinced that the only way to stop the student disruption was massive police intervention, virtually an occupation of the campus, by four hundred Buffalo city police. I was convinced this would be a catastrophic mistake, that it would destroy whatever legitimacy and trust the present administration tenuously held; that it would depress morale below the tolerable limits; and, finally, that it would be playing into the hands of the most militant students, who badly needed another clumsy overreaction by the

administration to keep their cause alive. Calling in four hundred
police was the surest way to "radicalize" the majority of moderate
students into joining the usually thin ranks of committed revolu-
tionaries—at Buffalo, no more than a hundred or so students out of
the 24,000 student body.

For these and other reasons, I had argued vehemently but
unsuccessfully against the police intervention. When I left Buffalo,
the police were expected to move onto the campus twenty-four hours
later, Sunday morning, March 8. My only hope—or rationalization
—in leaving town was that the acting president would recover from
this lapse of judgment when he could get some sleep, and when he
was no longer involved in a "win-lose" argument with me, the
number-two man at Buffalo.

All these things were on my mind when I finally met my
Booz, Allen contact at O'Hare Airport, at 7:30 A.M., Chicago time.
He escorted me directly into the chauffeured Cadillac owned by the
search committee chairman and drove to the chairman's house for
coffee. On the way, I was shown the schedule for the day. It was
more clogged than usual because I had insisted (and everyone fully
understood) that conditions at Buffalo were such that I could spend
only one day for this visit. After coffee, I was to be driven over to
the president's house for a two-hour talk with Rocky Miller. Then
the chairman would pick me up just before noon and drive me out
to the Glenview Country Club, where I would have lunch with a
group of about ten trustees. (Booz, Allen proposed a later meeting
with several absent trustees in Palm Beach.) Following lunch, I
would meet with the two faculty committees who had insisted on
the opportunity to interview and register their responses to all
"serious" candidates. Following that, I would have dinner with all
those faculty and student members of the search committee who had
not been able to come to Buffalo in February. This series of meetings would last through 9 P.M., allowing just time enough to return
to O'Hare for the 10:05 P.M. flight back to Buffalo.

The man from Booz, Allen was clearly glad to see me. He
told me that the search was down to four candidates, "two insiders
and two outsiders." This was more information than I had expected,
though I had heard that Northwestern's dean of arts and sciences,
Robert Strotz, was a very strong contender. I was also startled when

the Booz, Allen man mentioned the name of the other inside candidate, a man whom *I* was trying to recruit for a top administrative post at Buffalo. When I said that we, too, were interested in him, my Booz, Allen contact seemed both surprised and annoyed. "Haven't you guys looked seriously into his record here? Haven't you called anybody from Northwestern about him?" I replied that I wasn't on the search committee but I had every reason to believe that they had taken all the necessary steps, including informal "prowling," in their assessment. Our mutual candidate, it turned out, was the man responsible for the Northwestern "faculty intrusion" into the university's search for a new president. He was generally making life miserable for the search committee, which did not, of course, endear him to Booz, Allen. My internal radar, dormant throughout the lulling airplane trip, was suddenly reactivated by the inappropriateness of the Booz, Allen man's remarks. As he grumbled on about faculty troublemakers, the candidate began to sound better and better to me. (He eventually accepted the position at Buffalo.)

The day was predictably grueling. The two hours with President Miller were extremely cordial but basically a "nonevent." We spent most of our time in his car, driving around the campus. He pointed out buildings and told me what year they had gone up and which of the trustees had paid for them.

The two faculty meetings were condensed into one session, so I saw all twenty-five of the faculty at the same time. That was a good session, as I remember. The questions were sharp and incisive, and I was heartened by an intuitive feeling that they were looking for someone like me. The dinner with the four faculty and three students was also active, penetrating, and pleasant. In addition to the drama and speech dean, who left early, the other faculty members included Raymond Mack, a first-rate sociologist and head of the Northwestern Urban Center, and the faculty from the technology institute and the health science areas. I sensed very keen support from the students, moderate to strong support from the faculty.

Lunch at the country club provided the one remarkable moment of the day. It was a beautiful early spring day, with an eclipse that threw the bare-limbed trees into relief in sunlight that was both strong and muted, as if filtered through the edge of a fingernail. At times, I could barely look through the windows because of the strange brightness of the light. About ten people were present, including the Booz, Allen man, the search committee chairman, and a representative of the Northwestern alumni organization. He was memorable because he was clearly the youngest in the group. The rest, with one exception, were in their fifties and over. But they were a handsome bunch of people, most of them extremely cordial.

After Bloody Marys and sherry, we sat down at the table. Just as I began attacking the fresh fruit cup, the person seated two seats to my left, I think the alumni representative, cleared his throat and floated a question down to me. I was tempted to let it pass, but he had evidently been working on that question a long time, and I thought—mistakenly, in retrospect—that taking a shot at it would get him over the embarrassment it seemed to cause him.

"Who," he asked, "do you think are the three greatest university presidents and why?"

I returned my spoon with a melon ball resting on it to the plate and said looking up into the oak beams, "Well, Howard Johnson of MIT, for one. In my view, he is the administrator-manager *par excellence*. And imagine overcoming a name like that."

That seemed to relax everybody, and I continued. "My second choice would have to be Kingman Brew—" At that point, somewhere between the "Brew" and the unuttered "ster," the man opposite me began to choke as if something were caught in his throat. Two red-jacketed waiters ran over to him and started pounding him on the back. This lasted a good thirty seconds, until he seemed to recover his breath. His breath but not his composure. As he came up into a vertical position for air, the man shouted something to me. I couldn't hear him, although he wasn't more than three and a half feet across the table from me, and as I leaned forward, the ball of honeydew that had stuck in his throat at the mention of Brewster left it at a muzzle velocity of at least one thousand feet per second and smashed against my forehead.

At the moment of impact, the Booz, Allen representative, seated directly to my right, kicked my leg, and I began to wonder if this was some kind of perverse stress test they gave to all candidates. As the waiter dried my face nervously, my red-faced assailant increased the volume. He screamed, choking again. "Did you say *Brewster?* Would *you* keep that idiot Coffin on your payroll?"

I ducked involuntarily and then replied, more dogmatically than I actually felt about the whole business, that, yes, the Reverend Coffin apparently serves an important purpose at Yale, despite his radical views, or at least Brewster thinks so, and furthermore, I'm not sure that Brewster has the power or right to countervene on what are basically faculty prerogatives, and . . ." My questioner's coughing had subsided to heavy breathing, but his face was still alarmingly red. A trustee seated at the head of the table asked in a commanding voice if I wouldn't turn to my third choice, and we continued, almost pleasantly, as if what had happened were a trifling *faux pas* that we had collectively agreed to ignore.

The "honeydew statement" aside, the Northwestern search to this point is more or less typical of how most universities go about selecting a new president. The only unusual feature, as noted earlier, was the use of an outside consulting firm to coordinate the search process. (Later on, this backfired.) Of the 2,500 or so accredited colleges in the United States, only the most parochial (say, Bob Jones University in South Carolina) would proceed on a presidential search without a faculty, student, and possibly an alumni committee, working with a small group of trustees.[3] Northwestern also had alumni representation on the board. When a community college is searching for a president, the committee almost always includes prominent members of the community.

The search that Harvard undertook before selecting Derek Bok to succeed Nathan Pusey may well emerge as the new model for selection processes, at least at major institutions. In April 1970, Harvard's Committee on Governance (appointed by President Pusey the previous September after the spring crisis) circulated a fifteen-page booklet, *Discussion Memorandum Concerning the Choice of a New President,* calling for the most thorough participation in a presidential search known to Harvard, and perhaps to

---

[3] According to one survey, in 1939 faculty were consulted in the selection of 29 per cent of the college presidents then in office. By 1955, that figure had risen to 47 per cent. By 1965, faculty were formally represented by a committee to advise the board in 65 per cent of the cases.

any campus. Aside from an incredible number of consultations with "key groups," both inside and outside the university, the Harvard Corporation started its search with the distribution of some 200,000 letters inviting suggestions for candidates from (among others) faculty members, students, key alumni, Nieman Fellows, and employees. This correspondence alone took almost the full time of a professional staff member with a large staff of assistants and clerks. That first step was only a small part of the total effort, which cost an estimated half million dollars. (By comparison, James Conant was selected after only one appearance before the total search committee, during which he gave a clear analysis of the man needed and urged the candidacy of one of his closest friends.)

In one magnificently prescient paragraph entitled "How might the foreseeable negative consequences be minimized?" the Harvard *Discussion Memorandum* lists five stumbling blocks that may cripple a search committee:

1. Sheer volume of work.

2. The selection process may divide and polarize rather than unify the university.

3. Candidates surviving the scrutiny of many diverse groups may be the same hackneyed names who always turn out to be unavailable [what I refer to as the "John Gardner" syndrome] or, among those who are available, they may be essentially "low-risk," mediocre candidates.

4. A "credibility gap" may occur between the search committee and various groups within and without the university over the extent to which their advice is being sincerely sought, objectively evaluated, and imaginatively interpreted.

5. Potential candidates may be alienated by premature publicity, gossip about their candidacy, and vigorous opposition, even if ill-informed and limited.

Northwestern's search process left none of these "negative consequences" unturned. In fact, it uncovered several "negative consequences" undreamt of in Harvard's list.

Quite often, especially if the university is prestigious, a good deal of publicity attends and sometimes complicates the search. In the Northwestern case, for example, the student newspaper, the

Daily Northwestern, managed somehow to obtain dossiers on each of the three finalists as well as their ranking, even though all search committee members were sworn to secrecy and the candidates themselves are usually in no mood to discuss the race. For obvious reasons. No one wants to win honorable mention in a presidential search, even by earning a place on the short list. Active candidates try to appear majestically aloof from the politics of candidacy. Overt campaigning is as alien to the academic man, and as endemic, as it is to the College of Cardinals. All that is missing when a university picks a president is the puff of smoke.

The *Daily Northwestern* scoop of April 15, revealing the names of the three finalists (New York University's Chancellor Allan Cartter, Northwestern's Dean Robert Strotz, and me), was immediately picked up by all the Chicago dailies and in the hometown newspapers of the two outside candidates. The next day the student paper ran an editorial scoring the search committee for ignoring student opinion in the selection process so far. Everyone concerned refused to comment, although the leaked story was completely accurate—so accurate, as a matter of fact, that one candidate decided to withdraw from the race shortly after the story appeared.

Because of bad weather, my return to Buffalo after the Northwestern interview was delayed. I finally landed at Buffalo International late Sunday morning, March 8, and rushed over to the troubled campus to learn what was going on. The entire perimeter of the campus was surrounded, bumper to bumper, with Buffalo city police vehicles. Acting President Regan had called a noon meeting of all faculty, student, and administrative officers, and as I walked into the building where the meeting was to be held, policemen were already marching across the campus, army-style, twelve to sixteen per group in columns of two. When I arrived, Acting President Regan was explaining his reasons for calling the police onto the campus, a speech greeted for the most part with a lobotomized silence. Only three people spoke up. A top administrative officer said, "It's about time," and a faculty senate member who supported Dr. Regan's action reported that his department would "certainly support the police action." The acting president of the student association said that he and the other students were

totally against the police occupation and that he was even more
thoroughly disgusted with the acting president for going back on
his word that students would be consulted on all decisions related
to police intervention. The meeting dissolved after the student's
statement.

Afterward, I walked with Dr. Regan to a nearby office and
told him that I intended to resign as Buffalo's acting executive vice
president, not only to disassociate myself from the police intervention but for other reasons that made my future cooperation with his
administration impossible.

I wrote my resignation that evening (retaining my regular
post as vice president for academic development) and delivered it
personally to Regan the next morning, March 9. I was not totally
unaware of the consequences of the act and how it would be perceived, both inside and outside the university. If there were still
any doubts about the Northwestern presidency, I felt this act could
be interpreted, particularly by the Northwestern trustees, in any
number of unfavorable ways, from being "too permissive" or "soft
on law and order" to "desertion." My fears were confirmed during
the next few months in a series of unusual exchanges with Northwestern.

On Wednesday, March 11 (the day after the story of my
resignation had appeared in the *New York Times*), the Booz, Allen
representative called to say that the meeting tentatively arranged for
Palm Beach, Florida, during which I was supposed to meet a contingent of Northwestern trustees who spend the winter there, had
been canceled. He also pumped me about the resignation, clearly
trying to establish the background for my decision. Before the conversation ended, he assured me that he would "keep in touch."
Around the end of the month, having heard nothing in the mean-
time, I phoned him to find out how things were progressing with
the search. He seemed very flustered and said that things were in
a mess and that he didn't have any news for me yet. He said that
he wished he had never got involved "in this mess" and that he
hoped to have a chat with me, "man to man, after this whole thing
blows over." I thanked him and hung up, wondering what was
really going on.

So, apparently, did the *Daily Northwestern*. An editorial in

late April criticized the board for retaining, presumably at substantial cost, a management-consulting firm whose senior partner,
James Allen, also happened to sit on both the Northwestern board
and the search committee.

Between late March and the first week in May, the only
news I received about the Northwestern candidacy came through
informal sources. A student journalist at Northwestern called to
extract a story from me and in the process related a good deal of
inside information. On the basis of a purloined copy of the complete
search committee proceedings and other leaks, she indicated that
the students and most of the faculty favored me but that the board of
trustees, ultimately responsible for naming the president, was, as
expected, polarized; that Robert Strotz, who had been at Northwestern for practically his entire academic life, was seen by the
board as the "safest" candidate; that Chancellor Cartter of NYU
was moderately acceptable to the board and some students but that
the faculty was opposed to him. (I heard in early May, from Booz,
Allen, that Cartter had withdrawn after this publicity upon the advice of his wife.)[4] The students were so upset about the prospect of
Strotz (for reasons unclear to me) that they intended to do everything possible to block his appointment and to insist that only
Cartter or I was acceptable. They intended to use all means necessary to delay, obstruct, and ultimately subvert the Strotz appointment. According to the girl, the students were not ecstatic about
Cartter but were sure that the faculty would blackball him. I was,
she thought, the candidate most likely.

I also heard, about this time, that the Northwestern trustees
were in touch with some of their opposite numbers, members of the
Buffalo council, establishment types for the most part, and that the
chairman of the Buffalo council was saying publicly that he had
inside information and "knew that Bennis was not going to be
appointed president of Northwestern." The precise nature and

[4] Publicity of any kind seems devastating to both the candidates and
the searching university. Yet leaks occur, more and more frequently. When the
names of five top candidates for president of a leading midwestern institution
were leaked and published, all five men withdrew within a week. There are
many reasons for their withdrawals I suppose: pride or anger at the "sloppi-
ness" of the searching institution or, in some cases, because the candidate was
negotiating without divulging his intent to his own institution.

frequency of communication between the two groups were not known to me. I did hear that there was a good deal, none of it particularly helpful to my Northwestern chances. Meanwhile, a strong contingent on the home campus began urging me to run for Buffalo's presidency against odds far greater than Northwestern held for me.

Sometime around mid-May, I decided, at the risk of seeming more eager than I really was, to call the chairman of the search committee directly, rather than going the Booz, Allen route. I called because two other universities were interested in "exploring" presidencies with me. I wanted to be certain that Northwestern was really out of the question before investing time and energy on other prospects.

The committee chairman was "tied up" and did not return my call. Booz, Allen's man called instead. If his mood in late March was disconsolate, he was practically teary on this occasion. He startled me by suggesting that I call the committee chairman. "Tell him that you want to withdraw," he advised after I remarked that I was getting concerned about the search's lack of progress, information, and the other spooky vicissitudes of the search process. I asked him what I would learn or gain by withdrawing my name at this point. "Well," he said, "this way they'll know you're really serious." "Is there any doubt about my *seriousness* at this point?" I asked. "Well, you never can tell. And it will serve them right."

My level of paranoia, usually low, was rising, along with increasing doubts about Northwestern. I did call the committee chairman back a few days later. He began by apologizing for not returning my call. Trying to get clear and direct information from him in person was difficult enough, but on the phone it was like trying to nail a chiffon pie to a wall. I did not mention my most recent conversation with Booz, Allen, nor did he. He finally said that the search was taking longer than they had expected but that I was still in the running. "Hang in there," he encouraged me.

In early July, I called Booz, Allen for the last time. Their man indicated that he really didn't know what was going on at this point but that I should consider myself "out of the running." The following day I received a call from the chairman of the search committee, who, to my amazement, informed me that I was still "a very active candidate" and that he hoped to have word for me no later than July 21 or 22. He also reported that he had just been elected president of the Northwestern board of trustees. In order to facilitate the whole search process and to select a president no later than the third week in July, when the full board (about forty members) had its regular meeting, he was going to meet individually with each trustee. I told him that I was leaving for Europe on the sixth of August for a month, but he assured me that I would hear from him no later than July 21.

I should have listened to Booz, Allen.

When my family and I sailed for Europe on August 6, I was still in the dark about the Northwestern selection. The committee chairman's promise of "getting in touch no later than July 21" never materialized. After the front-page hullabaloo over student opposition to Strotz, I wagered that the whole search process to date would be scrapped and revived only with the appointment of a new search committee.

In early September, I returned from Europe via Miami to give a talk at the American Psychological Association meetings. At a convention cocktail party, a vaguely familiar-looking man came over to me and reminded me that he was a member of one of the faculty groups at Northwestern who had interviewed me. "I'm just so sorry that you turned us down," he said. I wasn't sure how to respond to that gracious and tactful opener. So I said, "I appreciate your tact and graciousness, but I was never asked. Was it Strotz?" He said that it was.

To this day, I have not received official word from Northwestern concerning my candidacy or Strotz's appointment—not from the search committee or from Booz, Allen. Finally, I sent the following letter to the committee chairman:

> When I returned from Europe on the 7th of September I quite by accident heard that Dr. Strotz was appointed president of Northwestern University. For any number of reasons, I am certain that you are delighted that the search is over and that you have found a first-rate person to lead Northwestern at this point. I congratulate you and the board on its choice and wish you the very best of luck—which all of us will be needing—in the years ahead.
>
> In light of my own candidacy for the post, I wonder if you

could write me a note, totally off the record, that would help me understand the reasons for the board's final selection. Obviously, I am aware that privileged communication and tact, and the usual practices, do not allow the frankest or most open discussion of this issue or the reasons why any candidate is chosen over any other, but I would like and would deeply appreciate "feedback" from you especially.

I might also say that I was surprised to hear the news in the manner I did. You had originally told me that you would be back in touch with me before I left the country. Since I did not hear from you through August 6, when I left with my family for Europe, I assumed that no decision would be made until I had been told.

Anyway, I would appreciate hearing from you whenever time permits.

Sincerely yours,
WARREN G. BENNIS

He never answered my letter.

3

The Buffalo Search

*W*hile Northwestern's search was muddling along, Buffalo was also looking for a new president. For almost the entire duration of the Buffalo search, from late February until the end of the academic year, the campus was racked by upheaval after upheaval, including a student strike, sporadic violence, a police occupation, and a mass arrest of faculty. The search process did not gain real momentum until April. By that time, finding a president seemed far less important than keeping the strife-ridden campus from any further explosion.

Since the university's founding in 1846, Buffalo has had ten full-time chief executives. The first, Millard Fillmore, who served as titular head of the university even during his brief tenure as thirteenth President of the United States (1850–1853), was named chancellor (as the presidents were called until 1962) for life. He was selected by a body of trustees, called "The University of Buffalo Council," formed by an act of the state legislature. The official selection process has changed remarkably little since Fillmore's day.

The official procedure for choosing a UB president is laid

down in the *Policies of the State University Board of Trustees,*
fleshed out by guidelines issued by the board in 1963. Final selection is to be made by the board, from a group of candidates win-
nowed down primarily by the university council—a body made up
of leading townsmen—with only an *advisory* role being played by
a faculty committee and *none* by students. Three or more candidates *must* be interviewed by both the council and the State University central administration in Albany before a final nomination
is made.

     With these guidelines in hand, the council and appropriate
university bodies began mobilizing to find a president. Less than a
week after President Meyerson's resignation in January 1970, the
search hit its first snag. On February 4, 1970, the executive committee of the UB faculty senate announced that the faculty committee advisory to the council in the search would consist of five
faculty chosen by the senate executive committee, an alumni representative, and three students—one to represent undergraduates, one
to represent graduates, and one for night students. Students immediately cried "Tokenism!" They complained that this apportion-
ment of search committee seats gave only *one* vote (and that merely
an advisory one) to 12,000 undergraduates.

     The student paper, *The Spectrum,* urged that students de-
mand and get five seats—parity with faculty—or refuse to sit on
the committee at all. At a meeting on February 9 of their polity,
the town-meeting assembly that was then the basic unit of student
governance at UB, the students voted overwhelmingly to reject the
faculty senate plan and to form an alternative search committee of
their own. As *The Spectrum* argued in support of this boycott, "All
the student power slogans, the debates over university governance,
the increase in student demands for self-determination of their
academic futures are reduced to nothing but empty rhetoric if students are willing to submit to token representation in the decision of
who will head the university."

     Students wanted to be heard in this search, especially so
because it was widely believed, rightly or not, that students at
Pennsylvania played what *The Spectrum* called "an active, if not
major" role in choosing Meyerson as president. UB students had
cause to be angry, but unfortunately their rival search committee

never got off the ground. Only seven students showed up at the first open meeting called to choose representatives. By the time the undergraduate and graduate student associations gave up the boycott late in April and took their seats with the official search committee, the philosophic basis for their holdout had become obscured by the flashier issues of the student strike, which then had the whole campus in turmoil. All that the boycott ultimately accomplished was to still the students' small voice in the selection procedure.

On the same day that the students voted not to join the advisory faculty committee, the UB council met to decide which of its members should sit on its subcommittee called "The Council Committee to Select a President." It named to this powerful subcommittee its own chairman and two other members, both UB alumni—all three western New York business executives. At this February 9 meeting, the council adopted a half-dozen criteria "for general guidance in the search." Most of these described an ideal candidate: He should be a recognized scholar with a doctorate, have previous successful university administrative experience and awareness of the role of a public university, evidence ability to conduct a large and expanding enterprise and interpret it to its many publics, be an effective speaker and writer and a person of social skills, and be in good health and between age thirty-five and fifty-five. The council also urged that the date of the SUNY board of trustees' meeting on April 29 be the target date for announcing UB's new president.

The role of the local council was an unusual feature of the Buffalo search. Local councils for the colleges and university centers of the state educational system were developed early in the history of State University of New York as a device to assure some degree of local control. They were seen as particularly vital to once private campuses like UB. At Buffalo, some of the trustees from the pre-1962 private university board were continued on as members of the council. The current chairman, William Baird, for example, who in 1970 had replaced retiring chairman Seymour Knox, had served on the old UB board of trustees for an uninterrupted term of some thirty years. (Baird recently retired as president of the Buffalo Pipe & Foundry Company.) All nine members of the council are appointed by the governor. They included the publisher of the

Courier-Express, two doctors, one dentist, three company presidents, a banker—a representative cross section from the most politically powerful institutions in the area.

Although the role of the local councils is ambiguous, especially vis-à-vis the chancellor's office and the board of trustees of SUNY, they are clearly mandated to nominate presidents for local campuses. Councils typically select a slate of candidates, making their favorite candidate known; then they present this slate to the SUNY board of trustees. In the twenty-five years of the SUNY system, no candidate nominated by a council has been turned down by the trustees. The only real power of the council is the crucial role it plays in presidential selection. But with the increasingly rapid turnover of presidents, this one function makes the council powerful indeed.

In the spring of 1970, the UB council was determined to wield its single option like a club. As Gerald Saltarelli, the newest and most powerful member of the council (one of the three council members on the university's search committee), said publicly, "This time, the UB council will submit one name and only one name to the board of trustees. And if they don't like it, then we'll resubmit it again and again until they accept it!"

This was the council's mood as it approached the search. The council was said to be fed up with "Albany interference." (In my own experience as an administrator, Albany usually tended to be protective of local autonomy.) The council had also had its fill, it was said, of the new style that Meyerson had epitomized at UB. During the Meyerson years, a steady influx of bright young faculty and a mass migration of New York students had increased both the standards and the national reputation of the university. To the Buffalo community, nostalgic for the days of a commuter university, the change was not necessarily for the better. The new look at Buffalo included long hair, pot, and radicalism. An old graduate back on campus for a pre-football cocktail party was liable to run into an Afro-coifed student selling Maoist literature. Many in the community were horrified. They longed for the days when local students denied admission to the eastern universities of their first choice were accepted instantly at UB. Now, a rising number of Buffalo applicants were being turned down, not only because of the

influx of bright New York City students, many of them Jewish
(stirring some ethnic animosity), but also because of an "open admissions" program, which seemed to give priority to black applicants
with poorer records than those that inexplicably made their own
children ineligible. Most of all, they were fed up with Martin
Meyerson and his administrative cohorts, men who had little
nostalgic fondness for or memory of the premerger university. Sharing many of these community attitudes, the council wanted a man
as president more in the mold of Meyerson's predecessor, the late
Cliff Furnas, a down-to-earth engineer (and one-time assistant
secretary of defense) with whom most of the council had shared a
comfortable, old-shoe friendship.

Members of the council reflected and gave voice to what
a large proportion of the town community felt deeply but could
articulate only obliquely. More surprising to me, a not inconsider-
able number of the UB faculty felt the same way. When I first came
to Buffalo, in 1967, I had construed faculty resistance to innovations proposed by Meyerson, or his appointees like myself, largely as
a reaction to change and as a function of the endemic antiau-
thoritarianism of universities. (Reluctance to accept changes can
also reflect honest differences of opinion, of course, and protects
campuses against faddism to some extent.) But the extent of the
university's anti-Meyersonian feeling became evident in the faculty
senate executive committee choices for the advisory search committee. With one exception, they were longtime members of the
faculty who were educationally conservative. Looking back, I suspect that these faculty wanted, perhaps even more fervently than
the council, a return to their nostalgic collective memory of the
campus of the early 1960s: quiet, peaceful, uncompetitive. In short,
the university's presidential search coincided with an intense anti-
Meyerson backlash from both town and gown.

The crisis mood of the campus heightened the polarized
atmosphere of the search. The local press and networks blared each
defiant student act, each faculty protest, each broken window. The
public was soon inflamed by such coverage. One morning the
Courier-Express ran an entire page of more than thirty angry
entries signed "a taxpayer." "Taxpayers" thanked Pennsylvania for
taking Meyerson off their hands and urged that "in our war on

pollution, perhaps we should first drain the cesspool of vice, drugs, and revolution on the UB campus." The university was everybody's political football. The mood was ugly. It was clear that the community itself wanted a hard-line, "law and order" president.

The academic community was not so sure what it wanted. Before the crisis began, the law faculty had publicly urged that an inside candidate be found in order to ensure continuity of the programs and policies of the Meyerson administration. By the end of March many faculty favored an outside candidate, fearing that an insider would be unable to reunify the campus because of animosities engendered by whatever stands he might have taken on the controversial issues of the strike. Toward the end of April, the *Buffalo Evening News* able education reporter Dan Hertzberg revealed that no decision could be reached in time for the April 29 target date. The faculty search committee, now with student representation at last, was considering more than seventy names, the *News* reported. One of them was my own.

By this time, I had reluctantly decided to become a candidate. Although an active and open campaign for office—any office —is infra dig on campus, academics who have spent time in business or public life invariably remark that university politics make other kinds seem as fierce as shuffleboard. During a period of presidential succession it achieves a secretiveness and subtlety that would have shocked the Byzantines.

Declaring for the UB presidency that April simply meant publicly admitting that I wanted the job, and saying, when asked, "I feel I can handle it, at least as well as any other inside candidate."

Before the crisis, I had been a strong backer of Acting President Peter Regan for the presidency. As his only visible possible rival, I felt that Regan was the more appropriate candidate for that particular time. It seemed to me that what the university most needed, following the spirited if spastic Meyerson years, was a "compleat bureaucrat" in the best sense: orderly, programmatic, practical, "savvy" about how to move large, complex human institutions. Regan had all these qualities. Moreover, I had a pet theory about leadership succession: Leaders come in two general types, conceptualists and operators. The former are best at breaking old patterns, at ungluing the status quo. They innovate, unfreeze, unsettle, and initiate. Aware of the importance of "operators" to complement their style, "conceptualists" make aggressive, demanding, visible, high-profile executives. Operators are best at consolidation, at developing coherence. More wary of their opposites than "conceptualists," "operators" work toward the semblance of stability. Meyerson, the innovator with bold, futuristic ideas, was often at a loss in implementing his dreams. I saw Regan as the consolidator who could realize many of the Meyerson goals still hanging in mid-air.

My own image for the job was not right for the times. I was seen as Meyerson's "prodigy" and protégé. His patina had rubbed off on me, for better or worse. Regan had been around before Meyerson, and many of the pre-Meyerson faculty saw him as one of them. For all these reasons, I saw Regan as the candidate whose hour had come. When a representative of the presidential search committee first questioned me about my possible interest in the job, I gave Regan my support.

The crisis changed my view. I was in fundamental disagreement with almost all of Regan's actions, and the massing of police on campus had clinched it.

Regan's actions caused others on campus to rethink their positions on the presidency. Early in April forty-nine members of an emergency-born University Survival Group, made up largely of senior faculty and department chairmen, urged Albany to hasten selection of a president who would have "the trust of both faculty and students as well as the outside community" and especially "the ability to act with even-handed restraint, sensitivity, and compassion in situations of crisis," a pointed reference to Regan's overreaction. The survival group also urged that adequate student participation in the selection procedure be guaranteed, and recommended that Albany obtain the advice and consent of a broad spectrum of faculty and students before making any final decision. "We are convinced," the statement concluded, "that it is vital for the peace of this campus and the success of the future presidency that faculty and students be extensively involved in the selection process." The statement could hardly have come at a time when Albany was less likely to listen nor did it enlarge the undemocratic selection process already prescribed. Albany did not respond.

No longer backing Regan, I nevertheless assumed my resignation precluded my running and disclaimed any intention to do so. Both Buffalo dailies front-paged my resignation. Although local television reported my comment that I was not running, nevertheless the resignation was seen in many quarters as a power play for the presidency. A politically astute friend, manager of one of Buffalo's media outlets, was bitterly angry with me when he read the resignation stories. He called me to say: "I thought that resignation bit was the smartest thing you ever did until I heard you say that you were still not a candidate. What the hell's wrong with you, Warren, resigning like that!"

"I'm really *not* a candidate," I told him. "I resigned because I thought it was the right thing to do."

After I decided to "declare" a short time later, my media friend called again. "Warren," he said joyfully, "I knew you had this in mind all the time. That resignation was the smartest thing you ever did."

I knew that my chances were slim, and initiating my own campaign was uncongenial to me. What tilted my ambivalence toward running was the fear that all the progress made under Meyerson would be lost. I was afraid that anti-Meyerson forces, both within and without the university, would turn the clock back to the uninspired "good old days." These fears deepened when I learned that a conservative caucus of UB faculty, in cooperation with many prominent townspeople, was strongly backing a new possibility for president. It was the former vice president for facilities planning, Robert L. Ketter, who had resigned abruptly in mid-1969 —all but openly blaming Meyerson for building delays on the new campus site. Ketter had been playing a leading role in the conservative caucus. If no other inside candidate materialized, and if the search committee could not come up with a distinguished outsider, then Ketter would be unopposed. If I still didn't have a call, at least I now perceived a mission.

Such images, quixotic as they now seem to me, do govern

one's choices. As a student of organizational behavior, I have come to realize that images are central to all our political processes. Images emerge in a complex and transactional way. People demand from their leaders, however unconsciously, an opportunity to externalize their deepest, most primitive dramas through identification, positive and negative, with men in power or aspirants to power. This subtle interplay and tension between the man and his constituents creates his "image."

The interplay was abundantly in evidence during the remaining weeks of the Buffalo search. Depending on which side of the "law and order" and/or Meyerson issue one stood, Ketter was "down to earth, sensible, straight-talking, strong, tough" or alternately, "rigid, anti-intellectual, vindictive, mediocre." Our audience could construct two equally polarized archetypes for me. My supporters depicted me as "liberal, humane, charismatic, a mediator, an administrator with some credibility with students, an idealist, a creative scholar." My detractors pictured me with equal ease as "permissive, disloyal, equivocal, dreamy, effete, soft on standards." (The "effete" image seemed to arise from a Tyrolean cape I sometimes wore around campus.) Crisis has a way of reinforcing these archetypes. In crisis, one cannot easily get feedback or, rather, can too easily ignore feedback that might jeopardize one's strongly held beliefs.

The immediate response to my announcement of candidacy was a flood of mail. Friends sent notes of encouragement. Many friends and colleagues endorsed me to the search committee and later to the local council and state trustees. Foes—all nonuniversity people except for a few alumni—sent hate mail. Several "spawn of the devil" letters arrived every week. Some were pasted together like ransom notes with letters cut from newspapers and depicted me as a Communist or Soviet agent, or both.

By mid-April it seemed appropriate to organize some kind of informal campaign. I gathered at my home a dozen or so colleagues and friends whose judgment I had relied on heavily as an administrator. They included faculty and administrators as well as townspeople I had become close to in my three years at Buffalo.

Also Mark Huddleston, acting president of the student association, and his predecessor, a politically astute black student, Bill Austin. Bruce Jackson, a brilliant young professor of English and folklore who had come to Buffalo from Harvard, became my informal campaign manager. My supporters represented a diverse set of the university's constituencies and shared most of my values, particularly on educational reform.

The strategy we devised was simple: (1) Consult the only member of the faculty search committee known to favor me. (2) Identify as much faculty support as possible and ask individual faculty to write letters to the search committee and the council on my behalf. (3) Get to any friendly members of the community who were close to members of the council and SUNY trustees. I was supposed to take a leading hand in this. (4) Articulate honestly and forthrightly, whenever and wherever possible, my own views.

Over the next two months, my work in my continuing role as academic vice president was largely sacrificed to presidential ambition. My conscience is clear, however, since UB was all but nonfunctioning, administratively, during the crisis. One wag said the only life in Hayes Hall, the main administration building, was "the frightful specter of waddling administrators, all out of breath, searching for new jobs."

From mid-April to early May, I was on a round-the-clock political schedule. My first hurdle was clear: I had to get the faculty committee advising the search committee to forward my name to the council as an eligible candidate. My own advisors saw as many faculty, students, and community people as they could and urged each of them to write letters of support, or personally see or phone faculty search committee advisers. We began to take stock. It was difficult to determine how broad my support was among the university's 1,500 faculty—or even where it was. We figured on strong support from the faculties of arts and letters and of social sciences and administration. The two groups accounted for almost half the total university faculty and also accounted for many of the most politically active faculty members.

As supporters, most of the professional schools, medicine and pharmacy particularly, had to be written off. The law school was split. The education faculty was splintered. Trying to make a "head count" was a futile exercise. Polling was out of the question. Many faculty wanted nothing more than to avoid the painful business of backing anybody—especially a candidate who had an excellent chance of losing. Most were praying—as indeed I had been until deciding to run—for a "distinguished outsider." My hunch was that in a popular election I might win by a very slender plurality. Of course, there wasn't going to be any popular election, and my most candid advisors told me that, given the existing mechanism for selection, I would fail. I thought so too. Still, we did think it essential to try.

According to the rules laid down by the state, student opinion was irrelevant. As it was, no candidate fired the imaginations of the students. Their "strike" preoccupied them, and they were also having governance squabbles among themselves. Neither Mark Huddleston nor Bill Austin could arouse the broad constituency that had elected them to take up my cause. They did draft a petition in my behalf, manage to get it signed by all student association officers, and sent it off to the council and the search committee. But the student body was not to be rallied. The general student body was recovering its collective breath from repeated confrontations with police. A few were too busy removing casts from legs or arms to care.

We decided that it was senseless to approach the community and the council until I was sure that my name had been actually forwarded to the Buffalo council by the faculty advisors to the search committee. Our reading of these five faculty members was not optimistic. The single ally we could count on was C. L. ("Joe") Barber, a relative newcomer to the university and a distinguished Shakespeare scholar. As we read it, two other members of the faculty committee were strongly opposed to my candidacy, one mildly opposed, and one perhaps neutral. I was certain that Barber would do his best for me, but he was spending the year in Palo Alto at the Ford Foundation behavioral science "think tank" and could attend very few search committee meetings. Worse, he flew off to Rome at about the time I became actively involved.

No one in our network of contacts could get any hard information on the workings of the search committee itself. Faculty members were taking their oaths of confidentiality with admirable seriousness. There were numerous rumors, of course, so contradictory they canceled each other out. As far as I could tell, everyone was in the dark. Dan Hertzberg of the *Buffalo Evening News* stopped in at Hayes Hall at least once a day, but there was little hard news to be had. We heard vague talk about the council: that almost to a man they preferred Ketter. Ketter had a routine administrative record and academic background. We reasoned that his only strength was with the educationally conservative members of the faculty, who saw him as a reliable plodder for the status quo. To many students and liberal faculty, his name had become a symbol of reaction. Since March 1, Ketter had served as head of the university's Temporary Hearing Commission on Campus Disruption, and his "Ketter Commission" had recommended the suspension of demonstrating students. Students regarded the Regan-named group as a "kangaroo court" usurping the authority of the student judiciary. Among the New Left on campus the Ketter Commission had about as much esteem as the Old Left had felt for Joe McCarthy's senate committee.[1] Previously a rather neutral figure, Ketter was now high on the radicals' list of administrative bad guys. But clearly his involvement in the suspension of radical students won him high regard in the Buffalo community, and it was community sentiment through the community-oriented council

---

[1] The nondemocratic establishment of the Ketter Commission disturbed many campus liberals and radicals, but the student judiciary had made itself unusually vulnerable to usurpation. Judiciary proceedings were overtly politicized. One February 1970 session ended with a shower of confetti to celebrate the birthday of Huey Newton. At the same session a liberal presidential assistant giving testimony was subjected to two hours of harassment by student defendants acting as their own counsel. "Do you know there are people on this campus training to kill you?" a defendant counsel asked him in cross-examination, adding that he was one of them. The judge-chairman protested recurring obscenity and abuse, but the faculty member who had been in the witness chair subsequently advised Acting President Regan: "Instructed by the realities of the situation, a simple question has formed in my mind: whether to move vigorously toward a new judicial system at the onset of the fall semester, or immediately."

that would decide the new president. We made the error of underestimating Ketter's strength. In the council, Gerald Saltarelli had reportedly talked other members into submitting Ketter's name to Chancellor Gould, who was said to have rejected it out of hand, having promised that UB would have as its next president someone of "national stature in the field of higher education."

The most bizarre rumor during this phase of the campaign was that Saltarelli, faced with Gould's rejection of Ketter, had submitted his own name. Gould was reported to have rejected this also.

From a variety of sources it was learned that thirty-five letters had been sent by the council to potential outside candidates and that only one had shown enough interest to visit the campus. The single interested party was a former Buffalo judge, William B. Lawless, who later became dean of Notre Dame's law school. I had never met Lawless but was delighted to learn of his interest, judging from what I had heard about him from his former colleagues at the Buffalo law school. I decided that if his candidacy materialized, I would withdraw my own name. According to newspaper reports, Lawless did spend time with the council on a morning in April and also visited Chancellor Gould. A few days later Lawless withdrew his name. He was reported to have told a friend living in Buffalo that he turned the job down flatly after speaking to the council. His reported grounds were that he did not want to "run the university like a prison warden—which is apparently what your council wants." The weeks of crisis were coming home to roost.

It did not take much imagination to figure out why no outside candidate wanted the job. No senior official in the SUNY system expected to be in office after the predicted Democratic sweep on Election Day. The state university's liberal chancellor, Samuel Gould, had already announced in mid-April his intention to resign. No one knew what the presumed new governor would have in mind in the way of appropriations for higher education. The Buffalo campus had a particularly indefinite future. Years after the target date, new campus construction was still not underway. After weeks of unrest, the campus looked less like the once-touted "jewel in the crown" of the state university system than a battered and harassed battleground. Green lumber covered every window in sight.

Rumors continued to fly that the names of from five to fifteen internal candidates had been forwarded to the search committee. Two names appeared on all these alleged lists: Ketter and Bennis.

Late in April, my media friend called to say there was going to be an announcement that day. Later a friend in the university's public relations office confirmed that the council was about to make its recommendation and that its choice was Ketter. No announcement actually came, but on the way to my Hayes Hall office that afternoon I saw the council members filing glumly out to their cars. Later I heard that they had been rebuffed that afternoon by Chancellor Gould in their bid to have Ketter named at once.

The final stage of the Buffalo search process coincided with the "seven days in May," the week when most of the nation's colleges were on "general strike" in reaction to the Cambodia–Kent State–Jackson State incursions. The effect of that week—including and perhaps especially Vice President Agnew's personal attack on Yale's Kingman Brewster, and the physical assaults by New York City "hardhats" on antiwar protesters—cannot be exaggerated. Many trustees, who in normal and more tranquil times could have been expected to represent a moderate liberal to conservative attitude toward potential candidates and college matters in general, became "politicized" and rigidly hawkish. One prominent member of the SUNY board of trustees said during this period, "What the Buffalo campus needs is a General Patton." (It's interesting to note that one of the favored candidates of the Wisconsin regents to replace resigned President Fred Harrington was General Westmoreland, the acting chief of staff. Their actual choice, former University of Missouri president Dr. John Carrier Weaver, was seen by many as a civilian surrogate of Patton or Westmoreland. The Buffalo *Courier-Express* noted in an editorial: "Wisconsin gets a hardliner.")

Whatever fragile hopes I had of winning plummeted during and just after the Cambodia–Kent State crisis. Anger at the news drove students off the campus and out into the streets of Buffalo. The Buffalo city police drove them back with sortie after sortie of tear and pepper gas. On one night during that long week, some one hundred Buffalo city and suburban Amherst police stood on the sidewalk on Buffalo's Main Street, a university boundary, lobbing cannisters of tear gas toward campus. My wife opened the window to find out what direction those dull and repetitive noises (like wet tennis balls hitting concrete) were coming from, then slammed it to protect herself from the fumes that swept across campus, over the golf course which separated our house from the university, and into the bucolic town of Amherst.

A publisher friend from New York had an eerie experience that night. The film Z was playing at a theater immediately across from the campus. Half dazed from the movie's powerful portrayal of life in a police state, he walked out onto Main Street only to see a hundred policemen firing tear gas across the front lawn of the university. The scene was so like those in the movie that he was temporarily unnerved and dropped to the sidewalk. Actually, the gas wasn't too bad at the theater. The wind favored that side of the street. After he pulled himself together, he began to wonder if the whole thing was not a staged happening. When I saw him next morning, he was still shaken.

For five straight days and nights the student-police confrontation continued. The daily denouement was a playback of the preceding night's, with a thousand or so students jamming into the student union and the police exploding cannisters of gas outside. The UB campus, never a very gentle or beautiful campus, began to look like a New York subway station. Judging from letters to the editor, and from the television and newspaper editorials, the community was now convinced that even a General Patton would have difficulty controlling what one local television editorialist called the "forces of anarchy so rampant in our once beloved UB."

A personally discouraging piece of news came to me indirectly at this time. One of my supporters, undergraduate dean Claude Welch, wrote to David Riesman, an inspirational friend whom I have admired since graduate school days, about the presi-

dential prospects for UB. Welch mentioned my name and that of
Dean Lawless as the only two "serious candidates." Riesman wrote
back that while he liked me, he thought Lawless, whom he did not
know, would be the better choice. "I have come to the conclusion in
the last several years that presidents in major universities in conservative locales—and which locale is now not conservative?—should
be conservative patricians. They can thus defend academic freedom
and they will not be regarded as betraying their liberal students
and faculty when they make compromises to keep the place alive.
. . . I would think that one needed a conservative president and
then underneath him an imaginative faculty and administration
whom he could protect. . . ." I wondered if Riesman might not be
right.

The first week in May my twin preoccupations were the
crisis and the campaign. My advisors now turned their attention
almost exclusively to the community and the UB council. I was on
the phone or in strategy meetings at least twelve hours a day. Eve-
nings I spent at the medical station at the student union. I would
leave the house at the first familiar pop of a gas cannister. My wife
would be watching by the door as I dashed out, usually with Bruce
Jackson or Mark Huddleston, all of us dressed in combinations of
ski clothes and army fatigues. It became a weird ritual, with Clurie
passing each of us a treated cloth to protect our noses and eyes as
we ran out the door.

I became a boarder in my own home, occasionally sleeping
in. Clurie, my durable frontier wife, only once looked sad enough
to cry. "Is anything wrong?" I asked her. "Am I too busy? Do you
mind being left alone? Do you mind my spending so little time with
the children?" "Oh, no, that's not it," she finally answered. "What
is it then?" "I'm afraid you're enjoying this too much."[2]

[2] The impact of the May experience on my children was another
story. One day in mid-July, when the whole business had ended, I took my
oldest child, Kate, who is six, to Boston to visit her closest friend. We went in
style, flying first class. As we were being served breakfast, I picked up the
Times. Kate asked me, pointing to the paper, if that was a picture of the
university. I couldn't see anything on the page vaguely resembling a university,
but Kate persisted. She was pointing to a picture of British troops in Ulster
firing tear gas from their barricades.

As university-community tensions mounted again, my campaign advisers expressed concern about my image with Buffalo's establishment. The wife of our family physician, an especially good friend of Clurie's, told her that "being seen in public with Warren is like being seen with Che Guevara." In normal times that remark would have been laughable to no one more than to radical students themselves. But in the public eye I was increasingly being cast as a "student lover," "power seeker," and even a "terrorist."

I went to see an esteemed and friendly member of the Buffalo community for guidance. Manly Fleischmann is senior partner of one of Buffalo's finer law firms and also one of western New York's two SUNY trustees. I didn't ask for nor did he offer me his support. He did provide friendly advice. He told me, as I was saying goodbye, that my qualifications, experience, and credentials made me the outstanding internal candidate. "But here," he said, and handed me a fistful of postcards. "These just arrived today. A batch of 75–100 come each week." There were about fifty cards and each of them contained the usual slurs, some bordering on anti-Semitism, most emphasizing my "permissive" and "radic-lib" tendencies. "We've all been getting them," he said, "All the members of the board and, I suspect, many others."

When I got back to the house, Manly was on the phone. He had meant to tell me earlier, but he had forgotten. "Look," he said, "if you want to be president of the university, you'd better not do anything publicly that links you to the Buffalo Forty-Five." Manly had just received an invitation to a lawn party Clurie and I were giving to raise money for the arrested faculty's defense fund. "We can't come," Manly said, "but whatever you do, avoid any publicity about your party. That'll kill your chances quicker than anything."

Social/fund-raising activities had been going on all spring for the defense of the forty-five faculty members indicted for occupying Hayes Hall in March in protest at the police occupation. Clurie and I planned a large party to precede another fund-raising activity for the forty-five, a concert of "Words and Music."

Even without Manly's warning, we had made no effort to publicize the party. But the next morning's Buffalo *Courier-Express* headlined it on the society page.

At least three hundred people attended that May 11 party. It was a social success and a political disaster. Almost all invitees from the university attended. Almost all invitees from the community were "going out of town" or "tied up." The airlines were oversold, judging from all the people "going out of town" that night. A surprising number of Buffalo friends phoned or wrote to say straightforwardly that (1) they did not want to be seen publicly supporting the forty-five but *would* send a check, or (2) they felt that by coming they would lend support to a dubious, most likely illegal, cause.

Weeks passed, and still no word came from the search committee. I was getting impatient, because of the possibility of the Northwestern job as well as another presidential possibility in New England. I was also growing concerned, as were my advisors, at the remarkable momentum building for Ketter. It was becoming clear that Gerald Saltarelli was going to be the "kingmaker" and that he wanted Ketter badly.

So I decided on the advice of a Buffalo friend to see Saltarelli. I called him on a Sunday afternoon and he set up a meeting for the following Wednesday. I had met him a number of times during my three years at Buffalo. I have always enjoyed being with him: he is aggressive, boisterous, direct, self-made, strong-willed, yet a vulnerable person. I always felt that he was a determined and decent man, not really snug yet in his worldly achievements.

I hoped to accomplish at least two things in meeting with him. I wanted to get straight, once and for all, whether I was a serious candidate. Second, I thought that if I had a chance to talk with him at greater length than in our previous social encounters, he could determine for himself, unfiltered through the press or television or postcards, what I was like. I reasoned that even if he did not agree with me on every point, at least he would find out that I am a law-abiding, loyal, and responsible citizen, none of which simple virtues the opposition was willing to grant me.

The day before the meeting, he called to say that the chairman of the UB council, William Baird, would be joining us. I arrived at Saltarelli's office on time at 4:30. Chairman Baird was already there and seated. Saltarelli was on the phone in an ante-room and didn't join us until about 5. In the interim, Baird and I exchanged niceties. Our conversation was kept on the level of sanitary chit-chat. Baird is a man hard to dislike. He is thoughtful, quiet, and constructive, scarcely capable of anger or high passion of any kind.

When Saltarelli finally finished his phone call and took a seat opposite me, Chairman Baird and I were discussing the "Buffalo Forty-Five." On hearing those supercharged numbers, Saltarelli went into a rage. "Goddam stupid faculty. Serves 'em right! And people like you who condone that kind of anarchy are just as bad!" That was for openers.

I tried to reply quietly. When Saltarelli stopped talking, it seemed as if the air conditioners had just gone off. I said that the Buffalo Forty-Five would have their day in court, that I was interested in their getting a fair trial, that that depended on raising a lot of money, and I wanted to help do that in any way I could. I also said that whatever the court eventually decided, I thought that the overreaction of the university administration had been stupid and that it played right into the hands of "those anarchists you seem so concerned about." Somehow the possibility of imprisonment for a peaceful "sit-in" in an unoccupied university office on a quiet Sunday morning after almost thirty straight days of terror seemed a bit stiff to me, despite the fact that I wouldn't have joined the forty-five if I had been asked. "Would you," I asked him, "respond to a sit-in in your office the way the university administration did? Wouldn't you have come down to your office to talk to the people, if they were *your* employees?"

That's how the interview went. Saltarelli would make a charge; I would respond. Baird sat absolutely still, not even having to move his eyes from opponent to opponent because we were leaning over the coffee table with our heads no more than six inches apart, like two tennis players at the net with racquets at port arms.

The entire hour and a half continued like a David Susskind show on "law and order." Saltarelli and I talked past each other most of the time. Baird was a passive observer. I was charged up and didn't care, at this point, whether I blew it or not. At about the half-time mark, I asked the two men whether this was an official candidate's interview. I think they said yes. Then, to change the metaphor, Saltarelli and I touched gloves and started in again.

The only points we did *not* cover were all the things on my mind when I decided to call him in the first place. Nor did we discuss whether or not I was interested in the job, what my educational and managerial philosophy was, or for that matter anything of consequence.

I learned later from a friend of Saltarelli's that he thought the interview was "worthless" and was quoted as saying, "I knew as much about him before we started as I did when it ended."

What I learned was that "search" had little to do with the search committee's function in the eyes of the council. By contrast, though Northwestern finally resorted to a board veto of student and faculty opinions, more than lip service was paid to faculty and student views in the process. The UB appointment was made with *no* significant student involvement and with the faculty playing a narrow "secretarial" role, merely forwarding eligible names to the council.

Perhaps only San Francisco State was more blatant than Buffalo in responding to the succession crisis without any important consultation with faculty or students, the individuals most directly affected by the decision. Robert Smith, former president of San Francisco State, tells about a call he received from Chancellor Dumke's assistant for personnel. "Bob, we're putting Summerskill out to pasture. We want you to come down to meet with the chancellor tomorrow morning." "But why should I come down?" Smith asked. Dumke's aide made it clear that the administration wanted Smith to become acting president immediately. Smith held out for a term appointment without the "acting" status and was appointed within a week.

Smith lasted for less than a year. He was replaced by S. I. Hayakawa. The Hayakawa appointment took place in an even shorter period of time and was handed down from even higher levels. As Lou Cannon writes:

Gov. Reagan and Alex Sheriffs, his educational adviser, had discussed the question of a replacement if Smith did quit and they had agreed that it should be someone from the faculty if possible. "I said we would be far better off if we found someone on the campus among the ranks because of the efforts of the radicals to make it appear that their autonomy was being invaded," Reagan recalls. "I said what about this man, Professor Hayakawa? I do not know the man but he has been quoted . . . as saying that the college should be kept open and all that."[3]

That story suggests another iron law of crisis: The more crisis, the more presidential succession; the more succession, the more autonomy the local unit loses. What we can learn from San Francisco State and from Buffalo is that *unchecked disruption leads to more external intervention at successively higher levels*, from council to trustees to governor. If at some future time our campuses again become violent, federal even White House intervention is possible. The threat to a truly free university presented by this pattern is staggering.

Search processes need not succumb to panic in crisis. During 1970, Stanford University endured as serious a campus upheaval as Buffalo, possibly as serious as San Francisco State's earlier disruption. President Kenneth Pitzer, a noted chemist who had come to Stanford less than two years before from the presidency of Rice, resigned unexpectedly in late June 1970. Ironically, John Gardner, in his speech at Pitzer's inauguration, had said: "We have now proven beyond reasonable argument that a university community can make life unlivable for a president. We make him the scapegoat for every failure of society. . . . We can fight so savagely among ourselves that he is clawed to ribbons in the process. We have yet to prove that we can provide the kind of atmosphere in which a good man can survive."

With only three months to go until the beginning of the 1971 academic year, Stanford designed and implemented a truly monumental search process, which should be a model for all uni-

[3] *Ronnie and Jesse: A Political Odyssey* (Garden City, N.Y.: Doubleday, 1969), p. 252.

versities, certainly those concerned with academic freedom, due
process, and broad participation. Serious candidates were interviewed by groups representing every important university constituency: faculty, students, alumni, trustees. Out of these interviews
grew a consensus. Richard W. Lyman, Stanford's noted historian,
was chosen as Pitzer's successor because many of the people whose
lives would be touched by the new president wanted him. After the
choice was announced, the faculty advisory committee on the Stanford presidency distributed to the entire academic community a
six-page summary outlining each step of the selection process.

I think that President Lyman will have a successful tenure
in office, that he will be in office far longer than his predecessor
was, in spite of the impressive experience and credentials Pitzer
brought to the job. I am convinced that the new man starts from
a firm footing *if the search process is effective*. Pitzer faced a student "sit-in" in his office on the second day of his term because
student members of the search committee felt that their voice had
not been given proper weight. While no one can know how important this factor was in the subsequent events at Stanford, it is my
hunch that the effect was significant.

The Buffalo search ended without the strong sense of legitimacy and due process that marked Lyman's selection.

The April 29 target date had come and gone, and Buffalo
was still without permanent leadership. The violence of the first
week of May gave added urgency to finding a fulltime president.
Weeks before, in mid-March, the faculty senate voted no confidence
in Acting President Regan because of the police occupation. Many
other administrators, including myself, had resigned university
offices. Under considerable pressure, the state trustees were expected
to name Meyerson's successor no later than their regularly scheduled
meeting on June 24. Rumors grew that their choice would be
Robert Ketter.

As that meeting approached, twenty of the university's deans
and department chairmen signed a letter to Chancellor Gould
protesting Ketter's rumored imminent appointment.

By mid-June the question was closed. The council announced that Ketter was its choice. *The Spectrum,* the student daily, promptly termed Ketter "unacceptable" to the students. Buffalo's conservative voice, the *Courier-Express,* endorsed Ketter on June 22, following a lengthy *New York Times* analysis of the controversial nomination, in which Ketter was reported as saying, "It is time to get back to some semblance of order on the Buffalo campus."

On Tuesday, June 23, the day before the trustees' meeting, a group of provosts and deans were invited to council chairman Baird's Statler Hilton suite to meet with Ketter. In a privately circulated memo, a faculty member at that meeting recounted what happened.

Ketter opened by saying that he had been approached by the council subcommittee about two months before and had been instructed at that time not to talk to anyone about the interview or any other aspect of the presidency. He had not heard from the council again until late the previous week, when official word arrived that his appointment had been recommended to the trustees. Over the weekend he had met with the executive committee of the faculty senate and others; at that time, the present meeting with the provosts and deans had been proposed.

He said that the day before, June 22, he had gone to Albany, met for three hours with retiring Chancellor Gould, and subsequently for more than an hour with Vice Chancellor (later Chancellor) Ernest Boyer. Apparently, Gould expressed regret that Ketter had been put in the middle between Albany and the council. Gould and Ketter agreed that the handling of the nomination had been unfortunate.

Ketter said that he had been told in Albany that UB had better straighten up or its budget would be jeopardized. This threat had apparently been transmitted to the state university central administration by leaders of the state legislature. Ketter said that Gould had advised him that when he became president he should appoint people to work with him whose absolute loyalty he could expect. A single policy should be pursued by his subordinates.

One of the deans and provosts asked Ketter how he would

handle things differently from Regan. He answered that he would be visible and that he would have called the police a week earlier than Regan did.

Ketter, asked if he thought the council's handling of the nomination procedure would make things difficult for him as president, shrugged his shoulders. Someone asked whether the trustees' final decision should not be delayed. Ketter answered that the university could not afford another acting president. He raised again Albany's warning that Buffalo must get its house in order or suffer economic reprisal.

Someone asked him what kind of university he would like to see. He said a place with "agitation and questioning."

He later commented that the university's poor image in the community must be reversed. He said the way to do this was to sell the "plus features and play down the negative features."

Ketter was asked again about the council. He seemed fairly unhappy about its attempt to usurp university autonomy but indicated that the council would continue to be important in administering the university. He pointed out that three council positions were open, and that he would be willing to see a student (over twenty-one) on the body.

When a few of the provosts suggested that he might not be the right man for the job, Ketter countered that others disagreed and said that he would do the best he could. He said that the trustees were meeting that night and that people who desired to do so should communicate their views to the board.

Afterward the provosts and deans met privately. The majority felt that the procedure by which Ketter had been chosen was not acceptable.

Bruce Jackson, my unofficial campaign manager, was a summer replacement on the faculty senate executive committee and had been close to the events of the past week or so before Ketter's appointment was made official. Another member of the executive committee told Bruce that the UB Council saw itself as management and the students and faculty as rank-and-file labor. The council saw no reason why they should be expected to confer with labor in a management decision. Bruce felt that the faculty search advisors had betrayed the trust put in them by members of the faculty. Functionally, they had done nothing more than put a wall of silence between the academic community and the council. The passivity of the faculty search committee advisors in the procedure had continued to puzzle me. It was explained later when a member of the faculty committee told a friend that Ketter was that committee's choice from the beginning. "We would have considered a nationally known external candidate," he said, but no other internal candidates were seriously considered. No one seemed to remember the rule prescribed by the trustees that at least three candidates must be interviewed in any search.

On June 24, the board of trustees officially named Robert L. Ketter the University of Buffalo's eleventh chief executive. The *New York Times* reported that Ketter had been unanimously nominated by the council although campus critics denounced him as a "law and order" candidate.

The *Times* added that John Charles, acting president of the UB student association, protested by letter to Chancellor Gould that the Ketter appointment "was jammed down our collective throats" and demonstrated the trustees' "total miscomprehension of campus tensions."

In an editorial the following Sunday the *Times* blasted the SUNY trustees for playing into the hands of extremists by settling on a "law and order" president.

Many members of the academic community—by no means limited to backers of my candidacy—complained to the trustees about the undemocratic procedure. All received in response the following form letter from the chairman of the SUNY board:

> I read each letter and telegram carefully and reported to the trustees the variety of opinions expressed. I had been impressed by the caliber and content of the communications—the deep concern for the future of the university, and the hope of creating the necessary climate for academic excellence.
>
> I assure you that the trustees join you in the determination that the university at Buffalo shall be not just the largest unit in the state university but one of the great intellectual centers for the

advancement and sharing of knowledge—and sometimes even wisdom.

We believe that the newly appointed president shares this vision and will do all that is humanly possible to attain it. But he will need your help. . . .

Dr. Ketter discussed with us his desire to open channels of communication with the various branches of the university family, so that he can listen and respond to the wide spectrum of ideas for improving the life of the university. I hope you will use those channels.

Above all, I hope that together we will surely build a great university.

More than a year after Ketter assumed office, many people were still angry. In mid-October 1970, the president appeared before the polity, the student assembly. Afterward *The Spectrum* reported on page 1:

Speaking with a double handicap of laryngitis and a hostile audience, President Robert Ketter attempted Monday to explain his position on various university matters to the student polity. . . .

In all, Dr. Ketter was called everything from a pig to a marshmallow. The meeting ended when his laryngitis became too bad to continue speaking, and when most of the students left the meeting. . . .

Students did not forget the tokenism of the original search committee. In a November 1970 editorial, *The Spectrum* made explicit the widely held feeling that Ketter was a president without legitimacy:

A search committee was formed at this university last spring to find a replacement for the departing president, Martin Meyerson. Student input was, however, totally ignored by that committee.

The man subsequently elected to the position by the board of trustees has found that he has absolutely no student constituency with which to work. Dr. Ketter has admitted with admirable candor that the process by which he was chosen left something to be desired. . . .

In any community it is the right of the governed to elect their own officials. It should be no different in a university community. This basic right must be extended to students.

What the students are saying is clear, and it speaks directly to State University of New York, whose official presidential search procedure still badly needs revision. It speaks to every institution seeking a president.

If controlling bodies insist upon dictating university presidents, instead of selecting men by more democratic processes, the campuses must expect resistance from all those excluded from the selection process. The president forced on a reluctant university accepts a job that is difficult in the best of times. If students or faculty perceive his appointment as coercive, his job becomes impossible. In these uncertain times, no president has *time* to spend winning over sulky constituents. I am convinced that no university president, hard-line, soft-line, whatever his style, can overcome the handicap of a peremptory appointment. A selection process that is not broadly representative hamstrings the man it settles on. Moreover, the process itself may become an explosive issue, as it did for Pitzer at Stanford.

There is a wider moral issue at stake here also, one that involves a university's commitment to the dignity of each of its members. The *Spectrum* editorial touches on it. John Dewey said it even more eloquently:

> No matter how ignorant any person is,
> there is one thing that he knows better than anybody else
> and that is where the shoes pinch on his own feet
> and that because it is the individual that knows his own troubles,
> even if he is not literate or sophisticated in other respects,
> the idea of democracy as opposed to any conception of aristocracy
> is that every individual must be consulted
> in such a way, actively not passively,
> that he himself becomes a part of the process of authority,
> of the process of social control,
> that his needs and wants have a chance to be registered
> in a way where they count
> in determining social policy.[4]

[4] Quoted in Corita Kent, *Damn Everything but the Circus* (New York: Holt, Rinehart and Winston, Inc., 1970).

The Search at Cincinnati

Late in November of 1970, I received a call from Cincinnati. The caller was M. R. Dodson, vice chairman of the board of directors at the University of Cincinnati and chairman of the committee searching for a successor to retiring president Walter C. Langsam. "Would you," Dodson asked, "like to visit the University of Cincinnati as a presidential candidate?"

In the week before the winter break, I met on campus with members of the board of directors and with a few of the university's 35,000 students and 2,200 faculty. Four months later, on April 6, 1971, the board announced that I had been named the eighteenth president of the university.

The appointment was made shortly after my account of the Northwestern search had appeared in *Atlantic* (April 1971). A reporter at that first news conference had read the magazine piece and asked how the Cincinnati search differed from the others I had experienced. There were three major differences, I told him. The University of Cincinnati search committee provided candidates with a great deal of information about the university. A member of the search committee kept me informed at each step of the search process. And, of course, UC chose me.

There were other crucial differences as well. In finding a successor for its retiring president, Cincinnati faced many of the same problems that Buffalo, Northwestern, and other institutions were up against. UC had had a troubled spring that left the campus divided. But instead of aggravating conflicts, the UC search process ultimately emerged as a means by which faculty, students, and board were brought closer together.

Admittedly, almost everything about the Cincinnati search is sweet to me, but the UC procedure was, in fact, significantly more responsive than others I had seen firsthand.

The UC search committee was formed in September 1970. It consisted of board members, deans, faculty members, and students. During the next six months, the group screened nearly six hundred prospective candidates. In February the committee submitted three names, including my own, to the board.

When word got around campus early in April that the board was planning to name an acting president rather than select one of the names on the committee's short list, the UC student body mobilized. Ten thousand signatures, representing nearly a third of the student body, were collected in less than twenty-four hours and presented to the board with a petition urging the directors to name a president at once. Many of the students did not even know who the final candidates were. But, as the student newspaper reported, students had "complete faith in the search committee and its members." The board responded to the petitions with an immediate announcement.

The counterresponse of the students to the board's prompt recognition of their sense of urgency was sincere good will, something trustees too frequently find these days only outside the academic community. The students' *News Record* editorialized that all participants in the search deserved commendation. "Last, and certainly not least," the editorial ran, "the entire community must realize that the board of directors has taken the largest possible step toward reuniting all segments of a university community that had become separated as a result of disturbances last spring. While some scars of last spring may remain, we can all unite in common effort to achieve the highest possible levels of creative educational development at UC." Student body president Mike Dale also publicly congratulated the board, noting that the decision was a result of "commendable cooperation among the board of directors, the administration, faculty, alumni, and students of the University of Cincinnati." Faculty representative Wilbur R. Lester also praised the board for adopting a sound and proper selection procedure.

The Cincinnati search illustrates a premise that has threaded throughout the preceding chapters. A university's search for a president is never a neutral process. Done poorly, it tends to further polarize a campus, to demarcate more rigidly the barriers between trustees and faculty, faculty and students, campus and community. But when a search is responsive, when the needs and desires of *all* the constituencies involved are at least acknowledged, the search process succeeds in much more than producing a warm body to fill the president's chair. It serves also as a vehicle for community building, for healing wounds and lessening estrangements. In order to have this beneficial effect, a search need only be good; it need not be perfect. The overall fairness of the search is what counts. And this holds true, given reasonable candidates, regardless of the individual finally chosen by the procedure. As lavish as campus and community spokesmen were in praising the UC board for its choice, many also commented that the search committee had found three well-qualified finalists, any of whom would make Cincinnati a good president. That is, no doubt, true because the search itself created the climate necessary for effective leadership.

4

The University Presidency: Search and Destroy

*D*uring months spent interviewing for presidential vacancies, I discovered that campuses seeking leadership are prone to a "search and destroy" syndrome. Enormous amounts of time, energy, and money are expended in canvassing the country for an ideal president, but the hard-found new man lasts only a few years before he steps down, and the university must begin to search again. Reasons for rapid turnover among university presidents are legion, from personal ambition to a sincere desire to return to academic work to such mundane but universal factors as fatigue and bad health. Today large universities are the antithesis of the walled sanctuaries of the past. Today's university is a high-pressure organization, and presidents can quickly burn themselves out. But while search and destroy is a fact of university life, it is not inevitable. The cycle can be broken and presidential mortality reduced.

Adapted from my article in the April 1971 issue of *Atlantic Monthly*.

There is no way, I am convinced, to turn back the clock, to make the president's job the comfortable, largely honorary position it has sometimes been in the past. Nor is that kind of regression desirable. Universities are tortured institutions at this particular time in history. Ideally, they are never completely tranquil. But the presidential chair need not be the hot seat it is today. By making certain necessary changes, a university can increase its chances of locating and keeping a capable president and creating an atmosphere in which he, as well as the other members of the university community, is able to work.

I have divided the following recommendations into two groups, those that apply to the presidential search process and those that apply when the new president takes office.

During the Search Process

1. *Remember that no single quality, trait, characteristic, style, or person guarantees presidential capability.* A century and a half of psychological research confirms this point. An Ivy League degree or a low profile is not in itself going to ensure the bearer of success in dealing with an adamant board, fiscal crises, or angry students. Being from the "outside" is no talisman either. The outsider may fail if he cannot quickly master the special terrain of his institution—fail just as dismally as the insider whose judgment is skewed by partisan loyalties held over from his prepresidential days. There is no one presidential "type," no presidential personality. In fact, the charismatic university presidents of the past—the giants like Eliot of Harvard—might have only mixed successes running one of today's large institutions. The time is past when a Stanford or a Columbia can be described as the lengthened shadow of any one man. It has been said that Henry Ford would not be able to get a job at the Ford Motor Company today because Ford now needs professional managers, not larger-than-life entrepreneurs. The contemporary university has also updated its leadership requirements.

In the selection of a university president, precedence must be given—over even the most seductive *curriculum vitae*—to the *fit* between a candidate's unique capacity and the needs of the institution. The search committee must ask itself some hard questions: What is the particular and idiosyncratic history of the institution (for example, has it recently experienced disruption or some other crisis and how serious was it); what are the institution's current needs; what were the characteristics and success of past presidents, particularly the most recent one; what are the economic, religious, political, and cultural conditions of the community outside the university?

With the specific requirements of the institution in mind, the search committee can begin considering various presidential styles. Many different approaches to university management have been successful in the recent past. Among possible presidential styles are the following:

The problem-solver/manager. This type of president tries primarily to identify problems (real problems, not temporal issues) and engage the best minds and most important constituencies to work on them. Howard Johnson, the past president of MIT, used this approach most successfully—for example, in his handling of MIT's near crisis in 1969 over the university's deep involvement with the military establishment. In the spring of 1969, *before* push had come to shove, Johnson suspended classes for a day and called a school-wide convocation to consider MIT's role in society. When tension began to build in the fall over the defense research issue, Johnson again met with as many students and faculty as possible to discuss ways in which MIT could redirect its resources away from military projects to research related to broader social needs. Johnson did call police onto campus at one point—but only after informing faculty that he intended to do so. Largely because of the president's skillful management, a violent confrontation was avoided at MIT— in spite of its unusual vulnerability because of long-standing relations with the Department of Defense research section.

The managerial style is often confused with that of *low-profile technocrat.* Similarities are superficial. Instead of putting the right people to work on the right problems, the technocrat tries to find *systems* that will somehow transcend human error (T. S. Eliot had someone like the technocrat in mind when he wrote of "those men who dreamed of systems so perfect that no man need be good.")" The concerns of the technocrat are all pragmatic. He cuts through moral and ideological dilemmas with a callousness that soon has students and faculty aligned against him.

The leader-mediator. Based on the labor-relations model, this style is just coming into its own. If one conceives of the university as a place where *any* decision is bound to please some constituents and alienate others, then this style is very effective. In fact, there may be no decent alternative. A number of men with industrial-relations backgrounds have recently become successful presidents—most notably, Robben Fleming at the University of Michigan. (Johnson also had a labor-relations background.) However, since the leader-mediator type of president cannot help but make one side on any issue angry, the accumulated anger eventually overtakes the good will. Therefore, the tenure of such a president is always problematical unless he possesses, in addition to mediating skills, a degree of charisma that keeps him personally above conflict. Skill at arbitration is especially valuable when the president finds his two most important constituencies, faculty and students, on opposing sides on some major campus issue.[1]

The collegiate manager. This is the style of the academic administrator in the strict sense of the term—the man whose primary commitment is to a scholarly discipline, who assumes the presidency as a faculty colleague rather than as a professional administrator. At those universities where the faculty voice is strong and getting stronger, we can expect to see presidential power gravitating more and more toward strong collegiate figures. These men are very like *representative* leaders. The model here is Parliament, with the faculty as the House of Commons and the board of trustees rather in the position of the House of Lords.

The advantages of this style are obvious, particularly in an institution that sees itself as, or aspires to be, a community of scholars. As McGeorge Bundy wrote recently in *Atlantic:* "[The

---

[1] The value of labor-relations experience to university presidents was apparently evident to the Harvard Corporation, which recently named Derek C. Bok as Harvard's twenty-fifth president. Bok, formerly dean of Harvard's law school, is an authority on labor law and was an arbitrator in several major disputes, including the Florida East Coast Railway dispute.

professors] want a man who speaks their language and hears them. They want a man who is just as good as they are—a man who deserves ungrudgingly the grudging respect they already give to his office. They need a man who is their kind of man, to act for them and for their colleagues." In practice, a man's academic successes and his ability to inspire the respect that most faculty reserve for excellent scholarship may not be terribly relevant to the day-to-day operation of a university. But collegiate management is likely to prevail in the most distinguished of our colleges and universities. A president of any other style is subject to a crisis of confidence among the faculty—a crisis that renders him all but impotent. As Samuel Gould, a fine chancellor who came to educational administration with only a manual for radio announcers on his list of scholarly publications, said (after announcing that he was stepping down as chancellor of the State University of New York): "It may be, as Paul Goodman suggests, that university administrators are becoming fit to do no more than sweep the establishment and then stand aside, genuflecting respectfully, while the faculty and students file past us into the halls of academe." Under such circumstances only a president who is also a faculty colleague is sure of a dispensation from genuflecting.

The collegiate manager is almost by definition an insider. If not currently on the faculty, he is usually an individual with past experience in the institution. William J. McGill, for example, came to Columbia after serving as Chancellor at the University of California, San Diego. But, as McGill told Columbia alumni,

Columbia was very good to me. I came here as a young assistant professor from MIT in 1956. . . . All the basic developments of my academic career took place at Columbia. Everything that I have come to cherish about the academic life was learned here. The principles of academic freedom, integrity, and responsibility that I sought to apply when I shook my finger under the noses of my colleagues on the faculty at San Diego, telling them how I thought a faculty should behave, are principles I learned from the Columbia faculty. All these things were given to me. There wasn't very much of me when I came to Columbia, but the standards of this institution made me a mature academic person. I owe this university everything that my later life has become, and

I want to repay that debt. I want to work to bring Columbia to the position of eminence in the new society that it has always held in the old society.[2]

The communal-tribal or postmodern leader. Leaders of this style are emerging in many of our institutions, not just universities. Paraphrasing John Tunney, the junior senator from California,

> I think we're moving into an era when our leaders will be tribal leaders; there'll be that kind of sensuousness and immediacy to the relationship between them and the people. People will have to know that a man is willing to lose everything, including his own life, to achieve what he believes in—and he will have to answer to that community. The people will have to sense that he'll take extraordinary gambles for that community. Bob Kennedy was really the first of these new tribal leaders, I feel. He had that mixture of romance and fatalism, mysticism. And there's no question there were deep and profound responses to him, responses beyond the conventional political equations. And I think that's because the most powerful dynamic at work in politics now is this search for community, and the man who can tap into this basic yearning will be the leader of the seventies.

The tribal leader—who usually heads a college, not a university—identifies strongly with students. He not only backs them; he often joins with them—whether on marches to Washington or on strike. He is himself an activist. John Coleman of Haverford is an example of this style. Evidence of a trend in this direction is that many recently elected college presidents are considerably younger than their predecessors. Harvard's Derek Bok is forty-one. Robert W. Fuller of Oberlin is thirty-five. The *Wunderkind* of higher education today—and the perfect example of the tribal-communal leader—is Leon Botstein, the twenty-four-year-old president of Franconia College in New Hampshire. Botstein, who has impeccable academic credentials, is candid and imaginative to a degree that shocks most older administrators. But Botstein's style is all but guaranteed to appeal to the unorthodox faculty and students at

[2] *Columbia Forum,* Summer 1970, p. 26.

Franconia. Asked by a reporter why he accepted the Franconia presidency, Botstein answered, "Because I'm crazy." All his public statements had an authentic "Cut the crap" quality that the young in this country clearly value—and rarely get from individuals in positions of authority.

The charismatic leader. John Summerskill, who preceded Robert Smith (who preceded S. I. Hayakawa) at San Francisco State, was a charismatic president, but the exemplar of this style is Kingman Brewster of Yale. Brewster's personal attractiveness transcends all obstacles: Yale's serious financial troubles, the escalation of town-gown tension in New Haven during the Black Panther trials, even the general campus malaise. As Derek Bok said respectfully of Brewster, he has had a unique success in being able to capture the enthusiasm of a great many undergraduates, at least in the sense of attachment to the institution at a time when great numbers of young people have had difficulty in developing that kind of commitment to college in general and to higher education.

In addition to these more or less acceptable presidential styles, several other possible approaches to university governance should be mentioned. The following styles are observable, and all of us have known men who practice them:

The "law and order" president. Hayakawa with his tam o'shanter and megaphone is the epitome of this style.

The absentee pluralist. This style, rapidly losing favor, has been highly regarded in the past. The president who adopts this approach sees his primary function as raising money for buildings and other needs and appointing competent subordinates. He hires what he considers to be good deans, spends his time on ceremonial functions, and "lets things happen." This is a spectacularly effective model if the university is rich, the subalterns effective, and the students and faculty relatively homogeneous and docile—in other words, if the campus mood is that of an elite men's club or the year is 1915. Faculty, even those who complain about "never seeing the president except at graduation," often like this style because it is best suited to their ideal of a university power structure; namely, legitimized anarchy, where the locus of decision-making is the individual professor. It is often less a style than the absence of one.

A president about to retire or a president with other major responsibilities (a government or professional commitment) may slip into this mode of operation.

The bureaucrat-entrepreneur. This style drives faculty to despair. The academic entrepreneur *par excellence* was Millard George Roberts, who with phenomenal *chutzpah* transformed a marginal sectarian college in the Midwest into a booming financial success and a national scandal. Before the bubble burst, Roberts succeeded in running Parsons College in Fairfield, Iowa, less like an academic institution than like a railroad. A *Swiss* railroad. The questions he asked himself and answered with a resounding yes were:

> Can you run a college like a business? Can you give economic considerations first priority in making academic decisions? Can you apply the principles of cost accounting to the instructional program? Can you put the curriculum on a production line? Can you get college professors to agree that "productivity" is something they ought to worry about and that their personal productivity, meaning the number of students they teach, should be measured? Can you suppress the faculty's normal preoccupation with its rights and privileges to the point that the institution's president can direct the institution's affairs like the chief executive of a major corporation? Can you inject free enterprise, the profit motive in particular, into higher education? And if you do, can you make a profit?[3]

Before he was run out of town and the college lost its accreditation, Roberts had created a highly profitable degree mill characterized by year-round operation; an open-door admissions policy; sharply restricted curriculum with large classes, heavy teaching loads, and high salaries (for some faculty as high as $50,000 with an apartment in New York City as a tax-free fringe benefit); high tuition and fees; and cheap, maximally utilized buildings.

Although Roberts is the stuff of which search committee nightmares are made, a toned-down profit-motive style of administration might be appropriate and could receive reluctant faculty acceptance at colleges where financial pressure is coupled with the current oversupply of professors.

[3] James D. Koerner, *The Parsons College Bubble* (New York: Basic Books, 1970), a moving and amusing account of Roberts' rise and fall.

When all else fails, and the search committee and board cannot reach agreement on any of the above presidential styles, there is always the *interregnum* solution. Interregnum leaders often do much better than might be expected. A recent historical study of popes, for example, reveals that interregnum popes achieved more in their shorter tenure than did "regnum" popes. A good secular example is Dr. Andrew Cordier, who surprised almost everybody with his able management at Columbia. The only difficulty with the *interregnum* solution is that good temporary men, like any other good men, are hard to find. Interregnum presidents have to be individuals who do not *really* covet the presidency, even unconsciously. Probably the only guarantee for this remarkable qualification is for such men to be near, if not at, mandatory retirement age. They must be able to subordinate their own desires, whether for professional development or family life or more leisure, to the requirements of the institution—without the assurance of long-term rewards. Ideally they have been around long enough to "know the territory" and yet be trusted by all constituencies. They must be competent without being threatening—probably a contradiction.

There is at least one other presidential style, that of the *Renaissance or protean man.* This is the elusive superman that so many search committees pursue, the man who is all things to all constituencies. Of all the approaches to university leadership, the protean style is the most seductive. Depending on the particular issue or situation, the protean president can role-play, presenting himself as a communal-tribal leader on some matters, a bureaucrat-entrepreneur on others, a problem-solver/manager on still others. On the rare occasion that one of these protean men is found, he can make life difficult for his constituents, who never know exactly what to expect from him. Such remarkable adaptability may even represent a form of low-level psychopathology.

2. *Determine the university's particular metaphor, the collectively held image of what the university is or could become.* Just as there are a number of successful presidential types, there are many university metaphors.

Metaphors have tremendous power to establish new social realities and to give life and meaning to what was formerly perceived only dimly and imprecisely. (What did adolescents experience before Erikson coined the term *identity crisis,* for example?) Most of us have internalized some metaphor about organizational life, however crude that model or vivid that utopia is (or how conscious or unconscious). This metaphor governs our perceptions of our social systems. (How these metaphors evolve is not clear, although Freud probably was not far off the mark when he suggested that the family, the military, and the church are the germinating institutions.)

Consider the role that a negative metaphor of university life played in the Berkeley Free Speech Movement. In a speech delivered on the steps of Sproul Hall, student leader Mario Savio spoke of the University of California at Berkeley as a terrible machine. Savio's image was perfect for the occasion. It gave that crowd of unhappy students a rallying point and helped weld them into a "movement" with a common view of reality. Besides the ring of truth, Savio's image had the virtue of being simple. An intricate analysis of Berkeley's problems might have left the crowd feeling powerless or at least forced it to act on many different fronts. By simplifying the issues, Savio made a plan of direct action possible. "The machine" could be stopped simply by massing warm bodies on the steps of Sproul Hall. Unconsciously, that negative image of the large university as a destructive machine has informed many of the most important developments of academic life since 1962, including the emergence of student power, the growth in importance of alternative educational institutions, and even the rise of the academic administrator, who is less likely than the professional manager to be perceived as a tool of the bosses.

There are many other more positive metaphors of university life. My first collegiate experience, at Antioch College, assumed a "community democracy" metaphor. In a relatively small organization like Antioch, it is possible to embody this metaphor in a town-meeting type of political structure. In marked contrast, the Massachusetts Institute of Technology employed the metaphor (not consciously, of course) of "the club." MIT was controlled tacitly—and quite democratically, though without the formal governing apparatus of political democracies—by an "old-boy network," composed of the senior tenured faculty and administration. Harvard also relies heavily on "the club" metaphor. The State University of

New York at Buffalo comes close, in my view, to a "labor-relations" metaphor; that is, conflicts and decisions are negotiated by various interest groups bargaining as partisans. Other usable metaphors are Clark Kerr's "City," Mark Hopkins' "student and teacher on opposite ends of a log," "general systems analysis," "therapeutic community," "scientific management," my own "temporary systems," and so on, competing with the pure form of bureaucracy.

3. *Forgo the costly hit-or-miss search and tailor the search to the special requirements of the individual university.* Once the university's metaphor—its collective self-image or ideal self—is determined, the type of president sought is automatically less problematical. A certain metaphor requires a certain kind of man. The search committee must try to find the candidate who best fits the metaphor collectively held or desired or needed by the university. A charismatic type is a winner at Yale, but he could easily be a failure at a state institution where the president must operate within a prescribed bureaucratic framework. The reverse is true, too. A manager type who does not also project a strong personal image would probably fail dismally in the Ivy League. Similarly, it is hard to imagine Leon Botstein or Gerald Witherspoon of Goddard as president of CCNY, for example. Timing is also a factor. Metaphors and institutional requirements change.

The university metaphor should determine not only the style of the president sought but also the composition and relative weighting of the search committee. For example, if a collegiate manager is sought, an individual with strong academic qualifications and faculty identification, then faculty should have the decisive voice on the search committee. If the university is seeking a communal-tribal type, students obviously should have more than token representation on the search committee. In any case, all constituencies should be represented. But the relative weighting of their inputs should depend on the university metaphor in combination with the leadership style sought. Whether a search is open—subject to public scrutiny at each step—or private also depends on this combination of key factors.

As a corollary to point 3, *a presidential search committee should undertake only an intelligently limited canvass, not a national quest.* When a university picked a new president every twenty years or so, it was reasonable to underwrite a far-flung search, sparing no effort or expense to screen all conceivable candidates. But the national search is beginning to appear as extravagant as the elaborate inauguration. It is almost obscene, in these days of tight money and real needs, to indulge in this kind of institutional ego-building exercise. Why should a university spend money and man hours contacting dozens of individuals—prominent government officials, for example—who are obviously unavailable or uninterested in a particular campus presidency? Short lists at least should be limited to persons known to be available. Similarly, serious consideration should be given only to candidates whose leadership style is known to be acceptable to all critical constituencies. Why pursue the radical scientist who is sure to be rejected by the trustees when other well-qualified individuals can garner support from faculty, students, *and* trustees?

The immediate benefits of a limited search are the savings in energy to the search committee and dollar savings to the university itself. Harvard's recent search is a conspicuous example of an inflationary search. It has been estimated that Harvard invested at least a half-million dollars in its year-long search for a successor to Nathan Pusey. An initial mailing of 203,000 letters was made to alumni, faculty, students, and employees asking for the names of possible candidates. (That the mailing list itself might have been more selective is obvious from the fact that the Harvard Corporation received only slightly more than 3,500 replies.) Given Harvard's unique place among American universities, it was predictable from the start that the Harvard Corporation would—no matter how far afield it searched—ultimately find a suitable president within the Yard. Derek Bok is eminently qualified to be the twenty-fifth president of Harvard; but with a bit more self-awareness at the beginning of its search, the university would have discovered that without spending a half-million dollars.

One obvious way for universities to limit intelligently the scope of the search process is to cull information from other institutions that have recently completed a successful search. Not every search need start from scratch. A search is a learning experience for the institution that undertakes it, and the lessons could profitably be shared.

4. *Finally, to meet growing demands for competent academic administrators, universities should develop rational career
development programs for promising young administrators.* Universities should be watchful for internal evidence of administrative
talent. On-the-job training programs for administrators would be
easiest to implement in large, diversified state education systems.
State University of New York, for example, has sixty-nine units,
from junior or community colleges to several multiversities. In
such a system, an administrator who demonstrates talent could
develop his administrative potential in a graduated program similar
to the executive-training programs set up by businesses. A person-
alized career trajectory could be devised for each "trainee": perhaps a vice presidency for finance or academic affairs at a four-year
college, then presidency of a community college or one of the four-
year units, then possibly a presidency at a university center.

In addition, courses in university organization and administration should be made available to everyone in the academic
community. At the very least, these courses can familiarize a larger
portion of the campus with the actual (as opposed to mythical)
operation of the organization.

When the New President Takes Office

The newly elected president usually enjoys a brief honeymoon, during which his colleagues and even the local press are care-
ful "to give him a chance," whatever reservations they may have
about him. This honeymoon period is critical for the new president.
During it he projects the image that his constituents will carry with
them—at least until their perceptions are modified by his management of whatever crises arise during his tenure. Ideally, this is a
period of grace (always with extreme accountability) during which
the president is given maximum freedom to prove himself. (Faculty
response in particular is crucial; when asked to list sources of
tension sixty presidents polled by the American Council on Education's Special Committee on Campus Tensions listed faculty first,
ahead of financial difficulties, problems of communication, and
student unrest.)

There are many ways for a university to prolong the hope-
fulness of a new administration's first days. The following recom-

mendations suggest several of these and also suggest ways to make
the termination process less traumatic for the institution:

1. *As soon as a new president takes office, all incumbent top
administrative officials should automatically turn in their resignations.* This is the very sensible practice in the diplomatic service.
If subordinate officials serve at the pleasure of the president, then a
new president should have the pleasure of reappointing those he
wishes to retain. Automatic resignation allows incumbents who
will eventually be replaced anyway to retire gracefully. It permits
the new president to devote his first months to problems more aca-
demically relevant than easing out administrators whose abilities
don't mesh with his administrative approach. Finally, it prevents
that awful purge mentality that can follow a change in administration (particularly a contested one). A new president must be given
the opportunity to bring in strategic replacements of his own choice.
These persons will work closely with him. They should be those
he values and trusts, not men with little or no personal loyalty to
him. A new president may even inherit a few disappointed internal
candidates for his position. Only the most saintly of these make
good subordinates.

2. *The president should insist upon a term appointment.*
Term appointments are a clear and welcome trend in higher education. They reflect, among other things, a changed attitude toward
career, a rejection by many talented people of the idea that one
locks into any one position, however satisfying, for life. The trend
also recognizes the rapidity with which skills and styles become
obsolete in contemporary society. Because of this—and because of
the enormous personal demands of the presidency—the appointment
should not exceed ten years. Brewster at Yale asked for and got
seven. In the middle of his term, the president's performance should
be reviewed (with appropriate feedback). This review is not bind-
ing; that is, it should not be used as a pretext for "resigning" a
controversial but competent executive. In general, a president
should retire at the end of his first or second "term."

There is another good reason for term appointments. In
these days of campus participatory democracy schemes, leaders are
often wrapped and smothered by a cocoon of extralegal procedures,
due process concerns, and confining and often worthless meetings

with governance groups that too frequently lead to shallow, distended, and bland decisions while destroying or discouraging leadership effectiveness—as well as the leaders. I feel strongly that the leader ought to be able to lead—that is, be given opportunities to act, to initiate, to take risks and embrace error without going through the time-wasting and useless contortions of a pseudodemocratic charade. Give presidents and all leaders a chance to succeed or fail. And give them some elbow room and freedom to lead, although not despotically. Hold the leaders accountable and throw the rascals out if they don't succeed in a reasonable period of time. Term appointments should facilitate strong, vigorous leadership, not diminish it. The review board should ask the president to continue only under extraordinary circumstances. This procedure would allow any individual president time to implement long-range plans and at the same time guarantee the institution a new administrative perspective at least every ten years.

3. *The president must develop an "executive constellation" to share the enormous responsibilities of university administration.* No university president today can manage, plan, set goals, develop systems of evaluation, work with outside constituencies, raise money, recruit, serve as a symbolic leader, and fulfill his multifarious other functions all by himself. Therefore, instead of trying to concentrate power in his office, the president should share his burden of responsibility by distributing responsibility among an "executive constellation"—deans, provosts, executive officers, vice presidents—who work with the president as an organic team. (Certainly, responsibilities and powers of members of the team, including the president, should be spelled out much more precisely than they now are.) This team must be more than a delegation; it must be an interrelated and complementary group of people who can deploy their energies and talents together.

4. *Boards of trustees can be very helpful to the president.* Often they are not, finding themselves trapped in the same day-to-day problems that the president attempts to avoid. There is a Bennis principle at work in all organizations: Routine work drives out nonroutine work. If a president of a university or any institution isn't strongly aware of this principle, he soon is sucked into spending all his time on the important but stifling and inevitably mundane

84

tasks of organizational maintenance. That is not leadership; that is administration. Leadership is the capacity to infuse new values and goals into the organization, to provide perspective on events and environments which, if unnoticed, can impose constraints on the institution. Leadership involves planning, auditing, communicating, relating to outside constituencies, insisting on the highest quality of performance and people, keeping an eye out for forces which may lead to or disable important reforms. Administration, as I use the term here, is managing given resources efficiently for a given mission. Leaders question the mission. Once the leader gets sucked into the incredibly strong undertow of routine work, he is no longer leading, he is following, which he is not paid to do.

Boards of trustees, as I say, often follow the Bennis principle by worrying more about the price of football tickets or security on campus than about the questions of leadership. They should ask only two questions of leadership: What are your goals? How do you demonstrate progress toward meeting these goals? The board can be a powerful influence in preserving the functions of leadership for the president, rather than by arrogating them or fogetting their true value.

Boards represent the crucial element, fiscal viability, not only in the university search process, but in the overall governance of the university. They must be active, policy-oriented, and genuinely helpful to and caring of the president without blinding themselves to his weaknesses. Trustees should probe rather than judge. And they should act as buffers, not conduits, between the campus and external (especially community) anxieties.

The accepted criteria for selecting trustees need revision. As Algo Henderson observes: "Board members too often are selected for their ability to make gifts. . . . Much as the money is needed, the policy seems unwise. It puts into the hands of persons chosen by a single criterion the governance of institutions in which there is a substantial public interest. Our colleges and universities deserve to be governed by persons who have been selected on grounds other than sheer expediency."[4] (In any case, public funds are now more

[4] *The Innovative Spirit* (San Francisco, Calif.: Jossey-Bass, 1970), p. 265.

important than private gifts in sustaining educational operations.)

In a recent study of university trustees, Ernest Boyer, now chancellor of SUNY, found that the median trustee is male, in his fifties (nationally more than a third are over sixty), white (fewer than 2 per cent are Negro), well educated, and financially well off (more than half have annual incomes exceeding $30,000). He may follow a prestige occupation, such as medicine, law, or education. Most probably, however, he is a business executive. Of Boyer's total sample, over 35 per cent are executives of manufacturing, merchandising, or investment firms; at private universities, nearly 50 per cent of the trustees hold such positions. As a group, they personify success in the puritan-ethic sense of that word.

Future board members must be more in tune with the students and faculty whose educational activities they oversee. This means more women, more blacks, more young people on boards. Because the value of a board is its "neutral" position between the university and the larger community, students and faculty and administrators probably should not serve on the board of their own university (recent graduates should, however). All board members, like presidents, should have term appointments.

5

Resigning:
A Bureaucrat's Dilemma

In speaking out one loses influence,
The chance for change by pleas and prayer is gone.
The chance to modify the devil's deeds
As critic from within is still my hope.
To quit the club! Be outside looking in!
This outsideness, this unfamiliar land,
From which few travellers ever get back in . . .
I fear to break; I'll work within for change.
*Macbird**

On March 9, 1970, the day after the police "peace-keeping" force arrived on the UB campus, I resigned as the university's acting executive vice president.

I intended the resignation to be a public protest against what I considered an unwarranted policy of force on the part of my administrative colleagues. The resignation dramatized, I hoped, my dissatisfaction with the handling of the troubles on campus so far.

* Barbara Garson (New York: Grove Press, 1967).

Personally, the resignation represented a turning point. For the first time in many years of organizational life, I was publicly dissociating myself from an institutional policy that I considered dangerous, even inflammatory. For the first time, I risked being an outsider rather than trying to work patiently within the system for change. It was a worthy cause, and I wish I could say that my resignation served as an effective protest. It did not. In some respects its limited success was my own fault. In retrospect, I realize that my break should have been total and that the statement I issued to the public explaining my position was an opaque disaster. But, personally unsatisfying as the act was, a record of it does shed light on the process by which dissent is neutralized in organizational settings.

The position I found myself in during the first days of March 1970 is one that many people working in large bureaucratic organizations recognize. They oppose some policy, and they quickly learn that bureaucracies do not tolerate dissent. What then? They have several options. They can capitulate. Or they can remain within the group and try to win the majority over to their own position, enduring the frustration and ambiguity that go with this option. Or they can resign. Remaining can be an excruciating experience of public loyalty masking private doubt. But what of resigning? Superficially, resignation seems an easy out; but it also has its dark and conflictful side. And if resigning is the choice, the problem of how to leave, silently or voicing one's position openly, still remains. These options are a universal feature of organizational life, and yet virtually nothing has been written on the dynamics of dissent in organizations.[1]

Acting President Regan and I had been growing apart on the issue of the police from the very beginning of the disorders in February. Until February UB had been an unsettled campus but

---

[1] The social sciences have surprisingly little to say about this topic. The only systematic and useful source I have found is a book by Harvard political economist Albert L. Hirschman. This book almost singlehandedly makes up for past deficiencies. Oddly enough, the book still remains "underground," largely unread by the wide audience touched by the processes Hirschman describes. Many of the ideas in this chapter were either suggested or inspired by this seminal work: *Exit, Voice and Loyalty* (Cambridge, Mass.: Harvard University Press, 1970).

not a violent one. Protest activities had centered on unresolved
issues raised in student protests across the country: defense and
other government-sponsored research on campus, ROTC, institutional racism, student participation in hiring and tenure decisions.
Then late in February the delicate balance of the campus was
tipped. The trouble started in an unlikely place—the campus gym.
On February 24 some three hundred demonstrators halted a
scheduled basketball match between UB and Stony Brook by
occupying the court. The action was to show support for black
athletes charging institutional racism in the UB athletic department.
The floor was cleared without incident, the game postponed. The
next night, however, a small group of forty or so demonstrators,
angered by the presence of Buffalo city police in the gym during the
previous night's action, rallied in the student union. They tried,
unsuccessfully, to meet with Regan in his office, where the acting
president was already involved in a late-night session on the racism
issue. On the way back to the union, someone threw a rock or snow-
ball through a window of Regan's office on the second floor of
Hayes Hall. More rocks were thrown, and campus police chased the
demonstrators back to the union. In the union things got ugly. On
the main floor a small crowd had gathered earlier that night for
the opening of a faculty photographer's new exhibit. Suddenly the
front doors burst open and students ran in, pursued by campus
police, clubs swinging. One student was caught by several campus
police, and an eye-witness later reported, "They went down on their
knees while he was face down on the floor, were hitting him on the
back of the neck and his shoulders." A crowd of students gathered
and watched the beating. Suddenly, it was the campus police who
were running, a dozen middle-aged men chased by some two
hundred enraged young witnesses. Things calmed down in the
union until shortly after 10 P.M., when the Buffalo police appeared
at both the front and back doors of the union and began moving in.
In the sweep that followed, twenty-seven people (including five
policemen) were injured seriously enough to need medical attention.
Within hours the entire campus was in a state of crisis.

    Buffalo city police had appeared on campus both on Febru-
ary 24 in the Clark Gym and again the following night when they
swept through the union. Who had called them? No one in the

administrative hierarchy claimed to know or admitted approving the call.[2] When I asked Regan about it after the Clark Gym intrusion, he said that there were no Buffalo police in Clark Gym that night; whoever told me that, he said, must have confused the uniforms of the campus security force with those of the city's tactical patrol unit. Regarding the February 25 police bust of the union, Regan told me that the city police entered the Union of their own accord.

Although I was nominally his number two man, Regan and I were, to some degree, an artificial administrative team. In the Meyerson administration, Regan and I were both vice presidents with somewhat parallel but quite separate responsibilities, although we had worked amicably together on such universitywide tasks as preparing budgets. When Meyerson went on two-thirds leave in September 1969[3] he turned most of his executive responsibilities over to Regan as acting president. At that time Meyerson, who remained in Buffalo and retained responsibility for long-range university planning, and Regan had asked me to serve as Regan's acting executive vice president while continuing to serve as academic vice president. Although Regan and I now had mutual concerns, he continued, understandably, to rely rather heavily on the group of colleagues and advisers he had developed as executive vice president.

On Friday, March 6, when I walked in—unexpected and

[2] In all fairness, no one, including Regan and myself, had any clear idea of what had happened the night of February 25 until much later. The campus police did not report the facts to us. In fact, we didn't learn that they had entered Norton Union until hours after, despite the fact that we spent most of that night in their headquarters and were in constant contact with them throughout the night. The tactical police unit was called onto campus by the campus police, not by any university administrator. At no time during the city police entry into Norton Union were we in the administration in control of the police. It's possible that others in the administration group that night were aware of the police bust, though I doubt it. A comprehensive picture was not available until a three-member faculty committee, appointed by Regan, distributed a report of "the events of February 25" (the so-called Griener Report) on March 8. As a result, all acts of the administration were made on the basis of incomplete or distorted data.

[3] Meyerson was on partial leave while heading a higher education task force (The American Assembly on Goals and Governance) for the American Academy of Arts and Sciences.

uninvited—on a meeting of Regan, the Buffalo police commissioner, and a handful of Regan's other administrative colleagues, I learned that the university administration was planning a round-the-clock patrol of the campus by nearly one third of the Buffalo police force. As Regan surely knew I would be, I was opposed.

Before the possibility of simply resigning ever occurred to me, I tried to change Regan's mind on using the police. We talked. We negotiated. Ultimately he would be convinced, I reasoned, if I did not push too hard. Whatever he personally wanted to do, my dissenting position would be a corrective factor in the final decision. Actually, at these meetings I was becoming the official devil's advocate, holding a titular position of virtually no real influence—a campus "Mr. Stop-the-Bombing," as Lyndon Johnson used to call his press secretary, Bill Moyers.

The strain of maintaining a loyal public face while my friends complained bitterly about the crisis management that I too opposed made the whole period, grim enough because of external events, a personal nightmare. A few friends urged me to resign, to disassociate myself from the Regan administration before it was too late. But I was convinced that the situation would deteriorate rapidly if I weren't "on board." A heady blend of naïveté and egotism led me square into the old "but-without-me-the-organization-would-go-from-bad-to-worse" trap.

Showing a public face unlike my private one was a new, unnerving experience. It struck me that one of the enormous virtues of candor is that it is less painful than alternative styles. But hateful as continuing the farce was, the idea of resigning frightened me. The chasm between the reformer, however difficult the task he sets for himself, and the rebel is simply enormous. I am not a rebel. My heterodoxy has never exceeded the limits tolerated by my academic peers. The growing difficulty of staying on and the fear of letting go put me on very shaky ground.

In my younger days, I would conjugate French verbs whenever I was frightened. In my current dilemma, I began to draw up mental lists of public figures who, against the advice of their friends, colleagues, and families, had served a government they disliked and had subsequently exerted enormous influence for good. I. Rabi, the physicist, came to mind often. When Eisenhower was elected in 1952, most of the government's scientific advisors, predominantly Stevenson supporters, left the government and returned to their universities. Not Rabi. He decided to stay. He felt, quite rightly as it turned out, that his leaving would deprive the government of its last authoritative and humane scientific voice. Leo Szilard and many others ostracized Rabi for his "defection." Rabi was vindicated several years later, when his evidence on the health-threatening effects of nuclear testing, dramatically presented to Eisenhower, persuaded the President to call for a two-year moratorium on nuclear testing. I thought of Rabi a lot. When thinking and the ambiguity of my position were too painful, I could race back into the marathon action of the striking campus. But at night I fell asleep with Rabi's presence always close by, like a security blanket.

On March 6, the day that I learned of the plan for a round-the-clock patrol of the campus, I knew I had to do something. With resignation still too threatening a course of action, I decided to *threaten* to resign. When I called Martin Meyerson for advice, he counseled me against it.

The next day, March 7, I flew to Northwestern University for the final round of presidential interviews described earlier. I flew back the same night on the last plane. Also on the flight was UB's undergraduate dean Claude Welch, returning from a conference. Halfway to Buffalo we learned that the airport was snowbound and our plane would have to land at Pittsburgh. Welch and I spent the night there, much of it in a passionate discussion of the events at Buffalo. He, too, felt that the use of force was escalating the conflict rather than limiting it. Toward midnight I told Welch that I simply could not support this most recent decision to bring police on campus as virtually an occupying force, and I assured him that I would not publicly endorse the move in any way.

I went to campus after we arrived home the next day. Usually Winspear Avenue's curb is lined bumper to bumper with the parked cars of university print-shop workers and maintenance employees. On this peaceful Sunday morning the parking spaces had been cleared for police vans, prowl cars, and K-9 wagons.

Walking across campus to the engineering building, where the meeting was to be held, I stopped twice to let squads of police go by. There were sixteen men and two dogs to a squad. They passed in double columns, the sun flashing off the visors of their plastic riot helmets.

Inside, Regan read a prepared statement explaining the presence of a "peace-keeping patrol." As soon as the meeting broke up, I walked over to Regan and asked to see him alone. It was close to noon. We found a small empty office nearby and sat down. I told Regan that I thought I ought to resign because I was opposed to the police presence and because of our growing lack of mutual trust. The meeting was friendly but inconclusive, with Regan attempting, it seemed to me, to minimize our differences.

Shortly after I got in, my mother called me to wish me a happy birthday. People began to drop over. Some friends from Buffalo, unrelated to the university troubles, dropped by with a gorgeous bottle of Bordeaux, wrapped in Christmas paper, with a loving card. They stayed to talk with some students and faculty who were commiserating with me about the unhappy turn of events. Almost everyone urged me to resign. As we talked, another visitor arrived. Konrad von Moltke, a young history professor and an administrative assistant to me in the academic affairs office, came in with a just-released copy of the administration-commissioned report on the strike-precipitating events of February 25. Konrad was one of the three authors of this so-called Griener Report. The report documented repeated instances of overreaction on the part of campus and city police and placed a significant share of the blame for the situation on the administration's lack of restraint in resorting to police in the first place. As we read the document, warning against the use of undue external force, four hundred police were marching around the campus.

I decided to write a public letter disassociating myself from the administration's decision. Bruce Jackson, a member of the English department and a trusted friend and advisor, came over to help me. Konrad and other friends who had dropped in stayed to talk, while Bruce and I worked on the draft. They drank the wine while we worked on a table in the kitchen. The mood was more and more that of a noisy wake as the house filled up with people, all wanting to sit close together and talk about the bad thing that was happening a few yards away on campus.

News came that there was a large, silent, and peaceful

march at the university protesting the police presence. Reports varied, but three to five thousand students and faculty had joined the march.

With Bruce, I worked on the protest letter until well into the morning. Several times, we called New York to consult Saul Touster, who had left UB to become provost and academic vice president at CCNY. By 3 A.M. I was barely awake. I left the draft with Bruce for a final stylistic polish. The next morning there was a note from Bruce on the bathroom door. "The letter's on the kitchen table. I went home to sleep."

By 8 A.M. I was on the phone again, reading the letter to Meyerson. He felt that simply protesting the police presence was not enough, that I should resign. He recommended that I resign the executive vice presidency but keep the academic affairs post. A protest resignation would strengthen the document, he advised; and retaining the academic affairs post would counter the charge that I was a "quitter." He also suggested some revisions in the wording of the letter.

I took the draft to my office in Hayes. The administration building, after two weeks of irregular occupation by striking students, had been cleared by police. Somewhat illogically I felt grateful to have my familiar office back.

Regan met in his office with his assistants each morning at 9. I walked the one flight up to his office at 9:30 or so. The meeting was breaking up. Regan greeted me, and I showed him the resignation. Regan was angry at first. Then his mood changed, and he asked me, in a warm and moving way, to reconsider, recalling how well we had worked together in the past. He was clearly tired and harassed on all sides, and I felt not a little guilty at adding to his personal burden by resigning, however sure I was that I was right. He suggested several changes in the draft, some of which I agreed to. Back in his office after the letter was retyped, the mood was calm and businesslike. He reread the letter with no more visible emotion than if it had been a memo to the maintenance staff that Lincoln's birthday would be celebrated on Monday that year. He did ask me to delay releasing the letter to the papers until he could draft a reply. At 3 I called his office to urge him to hurry with his statement and again at 4. Both times his secretary said he was un-

available. Finally, I told her that if I didn't hear from him immediately I would have to release the letter without his statement.
Minutes later the response was in my office.

The story was too late for the *Buffalo Evening News.* The
campus radio station picked it up first at about 5 P.M. The next
morning the *Courier-Express* headlined the story. The *New York
Times* ran a sizable inside story. That night I went to bed right after
dinner. For the first time in weeks, I slept without the ghost of Rabi
nearby.

Community interest in the resignation ran high for several
days. For the entire duration of the strike, any news from campus
was followed with the morbid fascination of war news. The full
texts of both my letter and Regan's response, reproduced here, were
widely disseminated.

Dear Peter:
    With sadness I want to disassociate myself from the admin-
istration's most recent decision to call the police on Sunday. I
believe that it is helpful in resolving our conflicts that the administration not be seen to be monolithic on these issues. It is for that
reason that I should like to make this letter public.

    I believe that the calling of the police on campus was pre-
mature because the administration had not bent itself, did not take
the necessary risks of self-exposure, to communicate. These are the
things I think we *must* recognize and acknowledge.

    1. If we had done ten days ago what we should have
done, we would not be in the situation we are in right now; to
assign all blame to an amorphous group of "radicals" is to avoid
admitting our own involvement in this awful escalation of force.

    2. Yesterday's bringing of the police undercut the adminis-
tration itself because it will be even more difficult to resolve any
of our problems after having experienced this atmosphere of
coercion.

    3. What started as a relatively small group of dissidents
has become a massive group of angry students and faculty. A
simple reading of recent history should have indicated that the
responses this administration chose would lead to such escalation.
We must recognize that whatever the various causes of this anger,
surely among the various components are the lack of perception,
accessibility, and compassion evidenced by this administration.

    I have just read the report prepared by Professors Chisolm,
Griener, and von Moltke, and I am moved by a terrible sense of

joint responsibility for these events. We were vulnerable to mistakes of fatigue, pressure, unpreparedness, and the self-doubt that prevents men from dissenting in crisis. But not to admit that we are susceptible to mistakes would be the most grievous mistake of all.

I write this as a member of this administration who is trying—as I know you have tried—to create an atmosphere of educational excellence and institutional security. I have been party to almost all important decisions made and had ample opportunity to register my thoughts. I also believe that you have made repeated efforts to prevent disruptions without the use of outside force. However, I believe that it would best serve the university and us if you would allow me to pursue a more independent role in thought and action as academic vice president and to accept my resignation as acting executive vice president.

Sincerely,

WARREN G. BENNIS

Dear Warren:

It is with deep and sincere regret that I received your letter of resignation as acting executive vice president. The last months have been satisfying and rewarding, as we have shared the responsibility for moving our university ahead in so many ways.

I can certainly appreciate the reasons for your wanting to be free at this time to concentrate exclusively on the area of academic development. The last twelve days have been painful ones. In an administrative organization dedicated to group process and to the forceful expression of divergent viewpoints, some of the decisions we have made have pained you, as well as myself. We have taken joint roles in those actions which were part of the painful experience of Wednesday, February 25, and in the many good and bad decisions which have been made since then.

I realize that the crux of the problem at this moment in time is the presence of police on the campus. Throughout the many discussions we had about this issue, we were both together on the central theme that every educational and positive thrust should be mounted, every peaceful means pursued, before police were brought to the campus. If there is a fundamental difference between us, it is clearly on the issue of whether or not the timing was right. In listening to your arguments that police action should be delayed until Wednesday, I had to consider two principal factors: the ineffectiveness of the positive educational efforts that we were able to mount during the past week under chaotic circumstances, and the confusion, demoralization, and fear which were gripping so many members of this academic community. In the end, I had to decide on the basis of my responsibility to protect, in every way possible, the rights of *all* members of the community.

I am grateful that you will be continuing to serve as vice president for academic development, in which position you will be able to work in a far freer fashion in pursuing those academic reforms which are so badly needed. Your advice and counsel has always been and will continue to be of great significance to all of us.

Sincerely,

PETER F. REGAN

Regan's letter, which I had not asked to read before it was released, came as a shock to me. He had chosen to diminish our basic disagreement to a question of timing. The clear implication of his letter was that I had publicly betrayed my colleagues after privately supporting their position. That was nonsense, and I indicated as much when asked about it by friends. Two days later, the matter was raised again in the press. On Wednesday the *Courier-Express* ran a statement by a "top UB administrator," claiming that I had supported Regan's decision and, indeed, had participated in a planning meeting on the matter on Saturday morning, March 7. I fired back a formal statement to the press that I had always been against the use of an external police patrol until such time as the university had failed in all its own peace-making measures. In that statement I made public the personally embarrassing information that I was out of town that Saturday morning (being interviewed at Northwestern) when the planning conference was held.

Immediately after the letters appeared in the paper Margy Meyerson called me to say that the exchange had had "just the right tone" and to share her relief that there had been no public recriminations or bitterness. Her relief was premature. The resignation was a disaster. It evoked a remarkably strong, generally negative response throughout the Buffalo community and on campus. I had half anticipated some community reaction, but the virulence of it surprised me. I began to collect hate mail, the classic stuff, unsigned and block-printed or patched together from words cut out of magazines. Along with the "nut-and-kook" mail was a flood of reasonable but impassioned letters from community members who were appalled that I had resigned and a great many phone calls from faculty who were angry because I hadn't resigned sooner. The same themes were repeated over and over in their communications: (1) a "loyal lieutenant" does not desert his "fleet or commander" during attack; (2) the resignation was blatant political (radiclib) betrayal, calculated to undermine Regan; (3) the resignation was a nefarious power play to unseat Regan so as to curry favor with radicals, students, and dissenting faculty and thus to advance myself as a candidate for the university presidency; (4) the resignation was at least "a week too late" (mostly from radical students and some faculty); (5) it was a hollow, grandstanding gesture.

What was most frustrating was the utter failure of the resignation to accomplish what I had hoped to do. As a consciousness-raising activity, it was a complete bust. It failed to call attention to the issues involved; notably, the importance of guarding university autonomy against injudicious use of external force and preserving an atmosphere in which the right to dissent is protected, even valued.

There were several reasons for the general nonsubstantive reading of the resignation. Buffalo was so highly "politicized" during the weeks of the strike that both campus and community people responded strongly and viscerally to almost any event on campus. The times were not conducive to close analysis. The search for a new president had further polarized the community. Given the highly charged atmosphere of a presidential search in the midst of campus crisis, many people felt that my resignation was a purely political move. Actually, I had not even considered becoming a candidate for the university presidency because of the hard-line mood of the Buffalo establishment. But many people attributed political motives to everything I did. In a sense they were right, because I later did decide to run. Besides, an exit during a time of crisis *is* a political act, no matter how much conscience is involved.

But the real clincher was my decision to resign only the executive vice presidency. Why, friends asked me for months, didn't I go all the way and resign both positions? How could I expect to use my resignation as an effective protest when in fact I hadn't given up my primary responsibility in the administration? Did I really expect that a fancy bit of fencestraddling could function as an effective protest? The distinction was obvious, I thought, between the academic affairs job and the acting executive vice presidency, a position involving responsibility for overall campus security, in which I was expected to serve as the alter ego of the president. Of course, it was *not* obvious, except to those within the administration itself. During a polarized, complicated, and confusing time, an act of dissent (especially when it involves a decision to retain one office and leave another) cannot be analyzed with the subtlety I had expected. What did I expect the public to be—detached and objective organizational theorists?

I had conceived of my exit, as much as I had thought it through, as a personal position, as an existential risk, even as an act of courage. I thought that the letter of resignation would clarify my situation and give support to many people who were confused and angry about the events taking place on campus. The intention was to be therapeutic, not politic. I never had any illusions that the resignation would enhance any of my career ambitions, especially for a college presidency. Rather, I viewed my resignation as a legitimate risk, one that I would undoubtedly repeat. By "legitimate risk" I mean that, given a choice, I would rather estrange myself from my institution than from my basic values, from myself. For me, resigning was a way, as Rilke writes, to restore the spirit "to its own most particular influence." It was a bid for personal survival.

Let me add to that high-minded analysis that—given my reference group, my friends, and the persons whose esteem I valued —my resigning was less an act of conscience than predictable, appropriate behavior. Morality is socially induced, after all, and the group of liberal faculty I most closely identified with was not exactly what one would call a "law and order" crowd. Later, when I did become a presidential candidate at Buffalo, this same reference group became my potential constituency. It was only then that I came to appreciate how subtly and inextricably the political is woven into any public display of conscience.

Looking back hard at the situation, I see that the *means* I used to express my disagreement all but guaranteed failure. This was partly owing to bad timing; in part, to inadequate or nonexistent deliberateness; most of all, however, it was the result of trying to express dissent in a passive rather than an active voice.

From virtually the first administrative decision during the crisis—when I passively agreed to cosign an evasive, blame-shifting administrative bulletin with Regan, rather than to confront the basic issues raised by the strike—I assumed the role of an "accommodating dissenter." Enmeshed by historically understandable, but nevertheless avoidable, traps, I rationalized myself into participating in and implicitly encouraging things to happen that I was deeply opposed to.

In the months that followed, I began almost by reflex to undertake a serious study of resignation and other expressions of dissent as organizational phenomena. I was fascinated to learn that, among American political figures in particular, resigning is almost never effectively used as a means of protest.

The garden-variety resignation is an innocuous act, no matter how righteously indignant the individual who tenders it. The act is made innocuous by a set of organization-serving conventions that few resignees are able (or even willing, for a variety of personal reasons) to break. When the properly socialized dissenter resigns, he tiptoes out. A news release is sent to the media on the letterhead of the departing one's superior: "I today accepted with regret the resignation of Mister/Doctor Y." This pro forma statement rings pure tin in the discerning ear, but this is the accepted ritual nonetheless. One retreats with a canopy of smiles, verbal bouquets, and exchanges, however insincere, of mutual respect. The last official duty of the departing one is to keep his mouth shut. The rules of play require that the last word goes to those who remain inside. The purpose served by this convention is a purely institutional one. Announcement of a resignation is usually a sign of disharmony and possibly real trouble within an organization (government agency, university, business corporation, or whatever). But, without candid follow-up by the individual making the sign, it is an empty gesture. The organization reasons, usually correctly, that the muffled troublemaker will soon be forgotten. With the irritant gone, the organization pursues its chosen course, subject only to the casual and untrained scrutiny of the general public.

A dramatic exception to this pattern is the case of Daniel Ellsberg. What is singular about Ellsberg is not that he became suspicious of the work in which he was engaged. What is unique is that he found a dramatic way to make his disagreement articulate. The organizational ethic is typically so strong that even those who dissent and opt for the outside by resigning do so with organization-serving discretion. Whether or not Ellsberg broke the law, he most certainly violated the code under which bureaucratic organizations function.

The striving of organizations for harmony is less a conscious program than a consequence of the structure of large organizations. Cohesiveness in such organizations results from a commonly held set of values, beliefs, norms, and attitudes. In other words, an organization is also an "appreciative system" in which those who do not share the common set, the common point of view, are by definition deviant, marginal, outsiders.

Ironically, this pervasive emphasis on harmony does not serve organizations particularly well. Unanimity leads rather quickly to stagnation, which, in turn, invites change by nonevolutionary means. The fact that the individual who sees things differently may be the institution's vital and only link with a new and more apt paradigm does not make the organization value him more. Most organizations would rather risk obsolescence than make room for the nonconformists in their midst. This is most true when such intolerance is most suicidal; that is, when the issues involved are of major importance (or when important people have taken a strong or personal position). On matters such as whether to name a new product "Corvair" or "Edsel," or establish a franchise in Peoria or Oshkosh, dissent is reasonably well tolerated, even welcomed, as a way of ensuring that the best of all possible alternatives is finally implemented. But when it comes to war and peace, life or death, growth or organizational stagnation, fighting or withdrawing, reform or status quo, dissent is typically seen as fearful. Exactly at that point in time when it is most necessary to consider the possible consequences of a wide range of alternatives, public show of consensus becomes an absolute value to be defended no matter what the human cost.

Unanimity, or at least its public show, is so valued within

the organizational context that it often carries more weight with
an individual than his own conscience. Thus, the *New York Times*
(March 31, 1971) notes that "Muskie regrets silence on war" and
wishes that he had made public as far back as 1965 his "real doubts
about involvement in the Vietnam war." Instead, he "voiced his
concerns privately to President Johnson." "There are two ways,"
he said, "and they're both legitimate ways of trying to influence
public policy. And I guess the tendency is, when the President is a
member of your own party and you're a senator, to try to express
your doubts directly to him, in order to give him a chance to get
the benefit of your views." Senator Muskie said he often had done
that, "but wish that I [had] expressed my doubts publicly at that
time." The article adds that Muskie "was far less hesitant to criti-
cize. President Nixon's conduct of the war." In an adjoining article,
Hubert Humphrey is reported as describing

> publicly for the first time the pressure he had been under from
> President Johnson not to speak out on the Vietnam issue. Many
> times during the first month of the campaign, he recalled, he had
> wanted to speak out more forcefully on the Vietnam issue only to
> be dissuaded by the President. This, he said, posed a personal
> dilemma. On the one side, he said, he saw his chances for winning
> the Presidency slipping away. But if he sought headlines on the
> Vietnam issue by taking a more critical stance, he said, he was
> being warned by the President that he would jeopardize the deli-
> cate negotiations then underway to bring South Vietnam and the
> Viet Cong to the Paris negotiating table.

"That's the God's truth. . . . How would you like to be in that
jam?" Humphrey asked the *Times* reporter.

Actually, Humphrey's "jam" is a classic one. A member in
good standing of an organization, in this case the Johnson administration, suddenly finds himself opposed to his superior and his
colleagues in regard to some policy. If the policy is relatively un-
important or not yet firm, the objection may be absorbed by bargaining or compromise. If the issue at stake is trivial, it may simply
be avoided. But if the issue is important and the dissenter adamant,
the gulf begins to widen. At first, the dissenter tries to exert all
possible influence over the others, tries to bring the others around.
In Hirschman's compact terminology, this is the option of *voice*.

Short of calling a press conference, the dissenter can exercise this option in several ways, from simply grumbling to threatening to resign. But usually the individual gives voice to his dissatisfaction in a series of private confrontations like those of Muskie and Humphrey with Johnson. When these fail, as they usually do, he must face the possibility of resigning (or, as Hirschman calls it, exercising the option to *exit*). Resigning becomes a reasonable alternative as soon as voice begins to fail. The individual realizes that hours of sincere, patient argument have come to nothing. He realizes that his influence within the organization is waning, and so probably is his loyalty. If he stays on, he risks becoming an organizational eunuch, an individual of no influence, publicly supporting a policy against his will, judgment, personal value system, at times even his professional code.

As bleak as this prospect is, exit on matters of principle is still a distinctly uncommon response to basic institutional conflict. This is particularly true of American politics. In many nations with parliamentary systems, principled resignation from high office is common. But in the United States the concept of exit as a political act has never taken hold. The Henry Wallaces and Walter Hickels are exceptions—and both their resignations were compelled. The last time a cabinet official left in protest and said why was when labor secretary Martin Durkin resigned because President Eisenhower refused to support his proposed amendments to the Taft-Hartley Act.

What accounts for our national reluctance to resign and our willingness, when forced to take the step, to settle for a "soft exit," without clamor, without a public statement of principle, and ideally without publicity? Tremendous institutional pressures and personal rationalizations work together to dissuade the dissident from exit in favor of voice. Most of us would much rather convince the boss or top group to see "reason." Resignation is defiant, an uncomfortable posture for most organization men (including politicians and academics). Worse, it smacks of failure, the worst of social diseases among the achievement-oriented. So instead of resigning, we reason to ourselves that the organization could go from bad to worse if we resigned. This may be the most seductive rationalization of all. Meanwhile, we have become more deeply implicated in the policy that we silently oppose, making extrication progressively more difficult.

If resignation cannot be avoided, there are selfish reasons for doing it quietly. Most resignees would like to work again. Speaking out is not likely to enhance one's marketability. A negative aura haunts the visibly angry resignee, while the individual who leaves a position ostensibly to return to business, family, teaching, or research reenters the job market without any such cloud. Many resignees prefer a low profile simply because they are aware that issues change. Why undermine one's future effectiveness by making a noisy but ineffectual stand? Whatever the individual's reason for resigning quietly, the organization reaps the major benefits. A decorous exit conceals the underlying dissension that prompted the resignation in the first place.

Like the Zen tea ceremony, resigning is a ritual in which how it is done becomes more important than the reasons for doing it. For example, when Fred Friendly resigned as president of CBS News in 1967 over the airing of Vietnam hearings, he sinned by releasing a news story *before* the chairman of the board, William S. Paley, could distribute his own release. Friendly writes in his memoir of this episode:

> Around two o'clock a colleague suggested that I should have called Paley, who was in Nassau, and personally read my [letter of resignation] to him over the phone. When I called Stanton to ask him if he had read my letter to the chairman, he said that he had just done so, and that Paley wanted me to call him. When I did, Paley wanted to know only if I had released my letter; when I told him that I had, all useful communication ceased. "You volunteered to me last week that you would not make a public announcement," he said. . . . The last thing the chairman said to me was: "Well, if you hadn't put out that letter, maybe we could still have done something." I answered that my letter was "after the fact, long after."[4]

Paley's response is explicable only if we remember that the *fact* of resignation and the *reasons* behind it are subordinated in the organizational scheme to the issue of institutional face-saving.

[4] *Due to Circumstances Beyond Our Control* (New York: Random House, 1967).

A frank resignation is regarded by the organization as an act of betrayal.

Because a discreet resignation amounts to no protest at all, a soft exit lifts the opprobrium of organizational deviation from the resignee. When Dean Acheson bowed out as undersecretary of the treasury in 1933 after a dispute with FDR over fiscal policy, his discretion was boundless and FDR was duly appreciative. Some years later, when another official left with less politesse, sending the White House a sharp criticism of the President's policies, Roosevelt returned the letter with the tart suggestion that the man ought to "ask Dean Acheson how a gentleman resigns."[5]

But "hard" or "soft," exit remains the option of last resort in organizational life. Remarkably the individual who is deeply opposed to some policy often opts for public acquiescence and private frustration. He may continue to voice his opposition to his colleagues, but they are able to neutralize his protest in various ways. Thus, we see George Ball becoming the official devil's advocate of the Johnson administration. As George E. Reedy, former White House press secretary, writes:

> During President Johnson's administration I watched George Ball play the role of devil's advocate with respect to foreign policy. The cabinet would meet and there would be an overwhelming report from Robert McNamara, another overwhelming report from Dean Rusk, another overwhelming report from McGeorge Bundy. Then five minutes would be set aside for George Ball to deliver his dissent, and because they expected him to dissent, they automatically discounted whatever he said. This strengthened them in their own convictions because the cabinet members could quite honestly say: "We heard both sides of this issue discussed." Well, they heard it with wax in their ears. I think that the moment you appoint an official devil's advocate you solidify the position he is arguing against.[6]

One can hardly imagine a predicament more excruciating than Ball's. Often an individual in such conflict with the rest of his organization simply removes himself—if not physically, then by shifting his concern from the issues to practical problems of

[5] *Time,* June 1, 1970, p. 16.
[6] *The Center Magazine,* 1970, 4(1), 12–13.

management and implementation. He distracts himself. This happened to many men of unquestioned personal moral character during the UB crisis. The question of whether or not it was politically, morally, and even practically "right" for the police occupation was converted into questions of logistics: How do we feed four hundred policemen? Can Clark Gym hold two hundred cots for those officers off duty? How do we provide church services for the men on Sunday morning? What about overtime? Who will pay for their services, the university or the city? On a loftier level, Townsend Hoopes suggests that Robert McNamara also occupied himself with practical details during the autumn of 1967, when the President and McNamara were growing further and further apart in their attitudes toward escalating the Vietnam war. Hoopes saw in McNamara the fatigue and loneliness of a man "in deep doubt" about the course the war was taking.

> *Owing to his own strict conception of loyalty to the President, McNamara found it officially necessary to deny all doubt and, by his silence, to discourage doubt in his professional associates and subordinates.* . . . The result of McNamara's ambivalence, however, was to create a situation of dreamlike unreality for those around him. *His staff meetings during this period were entirely barren affairs: a technical briefing, for example, on the growing strength of air defenses around Hanoi, but no debate on what this implied for the U. S. bombing effort, and never the slightest disclosure of what the President or the Secretary of State might consider the broad domestic and international implications to be.* It was an atmosphere that worked to neutralize those who were the natural supporters of his concerns about the war.[7]

What Hoopes (who was undersecretary of the air force at this time) describes is ethical short-circuiting. Conflict-torn McNamara busies himself with the minutiae of war planning because lists of numbers and cost estimates have a distracting if illusory moral neutrality. Toward the end of McNamara's tenure, according to Hoopes, the despairing secretary stopped questioning the military and political significance of whether to send 206,000 more troops into Indochina

---

[7] *The Limits of Intervention* (New York: David McKay, 1969), pp. 84–85. Emphasis added.

at Westmoreland's demand after the 1968 Tet offensive and con-
centrated solely on the logistical problems that would be involved
in getting them to the port of debarkation safely and efficiently.

Whether such activity exhausts an individual to the point of
moral numbness is questionable, but certainly the nature of the
large organization makes it possible for a McNamara, or for that
matter an Ellsberg (while at Rand), to work toward an ultimately
immoral end without an immediate sense of personal responsibility
or guilt. Organizations are by definition systems of increased differ-
entiation and specialization, and, thus, the morality of the organization is the morality of segmented acts. As Charles Reich observes,
"A scientist who is doing his specialized duty to further research
and knowledge develops a substance called napalm. Another special-
ist makes policy in the field of our nation's foreign affairs. A third
is concerned with the most modern weaponry. A fourth manu-
factures what the defense authorities require. A fifth drops napalm
from an airplane where he is told to do so." In this segmented environment, any one individual can easily develop tunnel vision,
concentrating on the task at hand, completing his task with a sense
of accomplishment, however sinister the collective result of all these
individual jobs well done. This segmented structure characteristic
of all large organizations encourages indifference and evasion of
responsibility.

How do intelligent, well-intentioned, educated men become
so caught up in a movement that they can accept what they privately deplore? Why don't they blow the whistle? Why don't they
resign?

A partial and rather misleading answer is loyalty. Loyalty
does undoubtedly play a role but usually an unconscious one. "Unconscious Loyalist Behavior" is the backbone of organizational life.
When evidencing "unconscious loyalist behavior," the individual
simply doesn't recognize his own disagreement; it is by definition
behavior free from discontent. It cannot lead to voice. As Hirschman describes it: "If, say, the likeness of a cat is made to change
gradually into that of a dog through a succession of images shown
to a subject and if later the same series is shown in reverse order,
the eye behaves as though it were 'loyal' to whatever figure it

started with: when the sequence is shown in the cat to dog direction, a majority of images will be labeled 'cat,' and vice versa."[8]

Loyalist behavior distorts perception. Albert Speer didn't *notice* Hitler's overly broad nose or his sallow face. He didn't *realize* until long afterward that Hitler's "whole face was repulsive." This perceptual distortion is one reason people typically don't resign at the "right time." They don't notice obvious organizational flaws soon enough. When they finally do, they have often become implicated themselves in the contested policy and can hardly exit as outraged innocents. One thinks immediately of Machiavelli's remark that political misjudgments are like tuberculosis, hard to detect and easy to cure in the beginning and easy to diagnose and very hard to cure at the end.

For McNamara, the ambiguity of his position eventually did lead him to consider resigning. Hoopes, however, provides a fascinating clue to McNamara's initial reluctance to resign or even to voice his uneasiness except in the most private talks with the President. In the following short portrait by Hoopes, we see McNamara wrestling with an ingrained organizational ethic stronger than his own intelligence and instinct:

> Accurately regarded by the press as the one moderate member of the inner circle, he continued to give full public support to the administration's policy, including specific endorsement of successive manpower infusions and progressively wider and heavier bombing efforts. Inside the Pentagon he seemed to discourage dissent among his staff associates by the simple tactic of being unreceptive to it; he observed, moreover, so strict a sense of privacy in his relationship with the President that he found it virtually impossible to report even to key subordinates what he was telling the President or what the President was saying and thinking. . . . All of this seemed to reflect a well-developed philosophy of executive management relationships, derived from his years in industry; its essence was the belief that a busy, overworked chairman of the board should be spared the burden of public differences among his senior vice presidents. Within such a framework, he could argue the case for moderation with the President—privately, selectively, and intermittently. But the unspoken corollary seemed to be that, whether or not his counsel of mod-

[8] Hirschman, p. 91.

eration were followed, there could arise no issue or difference
with President Johnson sufficient to require his resignation—
whether to enlighten public opinion or avoid personal stultifica-
tion. It was this corollary that seemed of doubtful applicability to
the problems and obligations of public office. *McNamara gave
evidence that he had ruled out resignation because he believed
that the situation would grow worse if he left the field to Rusk,
Rostow, and the joint chiefs. But also because the idea was so
strongly against the grain of his temperament and his considered
philosophy of organizational effectiveness.*[9]

Does this mean that McNamara would not resign because
quitting violated some personal notion of honor? Or does it mean
(as I suspect it does) that he regarded dissent and "organizational
effectiveness" as negatively correlated? Like any other corporation
president, McNamara was raised on organizational folklore. One
of the central myths is that the show of unanimity is always desirable. That this belief is false and even dangerous does not limit its
currency. There are times, of course, when discretion is required.
Clearly, organizations should not fight constantly in public. But
what is the gain of forbidding at all costs and at all times any
emotional give-and-take between colleagues? A man has an honest
difference of opinion with the organizational powers. Why must
he be silenced or domesticated or driven out so that the public can
continue to believe that organizational life is without strife? And
yet organizations continue to assume the most contrived postures
in order to maintain the illusion of harmony—postures like lying to
the public.

Our inability to transcend the dangerous notion that we
don't wash our dirty linen in public verges on the schizophrenic.
It implies not only that dissent is bad but that our public institutions
are made up not of men but of saints, who never engage in vulgar
and offensive activities. Thus, government strives to be regarded as
a hallowed shrine where, as George E. Reedy reports from his
White House experience, "the meanest lust for power can be sancti-
fied and the dullest wit greeted with reverential awe."[10] In fact,
organizations are vulgar, sweaty, plebeian; if they are to be viable,

---

[9] *Limits of Intervention*, p. 53. Emphasis added.

[10] *The Twilight of the Presidency* (New York: World Publishing
Company, 1970), pp. xxiv–xv.

they must create an institutional environment where a fool can be
called a fool and all actions and motivations are duly and closely
scrutinized for the inevitable human flaws and failures. In a democracy, meanness, dullness, and corruption are always amply represented. They are not entitled to protection from the same rude
challenges that such qualities must face in the "real" world. When
banal politeness is assigned a higher value than accountability or
truthfulness, the result is an Orwellian world where the symbols of
speech are manipulated to create false realities.

"Loyalty" is often given, as it was by critics of my own resignation, as a reason or pretext for muffling dissent. A variation on
this is the claim that candor "gives comfort to the enemy." Ellsberg's
national loyalty was repeatedly questioned in connection with his
release of the so-called Pentagon Papers. In the first three install-
ments of the document as run in the *Times,* practically nothing that
wasn't well known was revealed. A few details, an interesting admission or two, but basically nothing that had not come to light
earlier in other less controversial articles and books on the Indochina
war. But government officials trying to suppress the publication of
this classified material chose to make much of the "foreign consequences" of its release. "You may rest assured," a government
official was quoted as saying by the *Buffalo Evening News* (June
16, 1971), "that no one is reading this series any more closely
than the Soviet Embassy."

All of the foregoing pressures against registering dissent can
be subsumed under the clumsy label of "loyalty." In fact, they
represent much more subtle personal and organizational factors,
including deep-rooted psychological dependence, authority problems, simple ambition, cooptive mechanisms (the "devil's advocacy"
technique), pressure to be a member of the club and fear of being
outside looking in, adherence to the myth that gentlemen settle their
differences amicably and privately, fear of disloyalty in the form of
giving comfort to "the enemy," and, very often, that powerful
Prospero aspiration: the conviction that one's own "reasonable"
efforts will keep things from going from bad to worse.

There is a further broad cultural factor that must be considered before the other defenses against exit can be understood. It
simply doesn't make sense for a man as intelligent and analytically

sophisticated as our nation's "No. 1 problem solver," Robert
McNamara, to delude himself that he could not quit because "duty
called." Duty to whom? Not to his own principles? Nor, as he saw
it, to the nation's welfare. McNamara's real loyalty was to the
code of the "organizational society" in which most of us live out our
entire active careers. Ninety per cent of the employed population of
this country works in formal organizations. Status, position, a sense
of competence and accomplishment are all achieved in our culture
through belonging to these institutions. What you *do* determines, to
a large extent, what you *are*. "My son, the doctor" is not only the
punch line of a thousand Jewish jokes. It is a neat formulation of a
significant fact about our culture. Identification with a profession
or other organization is a real-life passport to identity, to selfhood,
to self-esteem. You are what you do, and work in our society (as in
all other industrialized societies) is done in large, complex bureaucratic structures. If one leaves the organization, particularly with
protest, one is nowhere, like a character in a Beckett play, without
role, without the props of office, without ambience or setting.

In fact, a few more resignations would be good for individual
consciences and good for the country. Looking back, veteran
diplomat Robert Murphy could recall only one occasion when he
thought he should have resigned. The single instance was the Berlin
Blockade of 1948–49, which he thought the United States should
have challenged more vigorously. "My resignation almost certainly
would not have affected events," he wrote in regret, "but if I had
resigned, I would feel better today about my own part in that episode." *Time* Magazine (June 1, 1970), from which Murphy's
quotation was taken, goes on to say in its essay: "In the long run,
the country would probably feel better, too, if a few more people
were ready to quit for their convictions. It might be a little unsettling, but it could have a tonic effect on American politics, for it
would give people the assurance that men who stay truly believe in
what they are doing."

I began this chapter by recounting my own attempt to
register dissent by resigning. One can ask: Weren't there other
options? The answer is, Yes. I could have shrieked, then instead of
now. I could have enlisted colleagues, Theodore Friend, Claude

Welch, and several others in the near-to-the-top administrative hierarchy who shared my view. We could have thrown a collective tantrum on Friday night, March 6. Too often, control of emotion becomes a cardinal virtue in its own right, and acting *appropriately* in the presence of one's fellow decision-makers becomes a higher priority than choosing the appropriate course of action. I certainly could have canceled the Northwestern trip, instead of indulging in abstruse "psychologizing" that my absence might bring Regan to his senses. I could have stayed around. I could have gone over Meyerson's head to Chancellor Gould, with whom I enjoyed a close and affectionate relationship. I could have threatened to resign long before I did in fact resign. I certainly should have recognized that my protest would be softened by my "equivocal exit" (holding one job and quitting the other).

But in the last analysis my reason for resigning was an intensely personal one. I did not want to say, a month or two months after the police came in, "Well, I was against that move at the time." I think it is important for everyone in decision-making positions in our institutions to speak out. And if we find it impossible to continue on as administrators because we are at total and continuous odds with institutional policy, then I think we must quit and go out shouting. The alternative is petit-Eichmannism, and it is too high a price.

6

The Berkeley of the East

My very first telephone call from Buffalo, on December 19, 1966, was from Saul Touster, an assistant to Martin Meyerson, a law professor, a poet, and chairman of the search committee that had lured Meyerson from his acting chancellorship at Berkeley in 1966. Touster began the conversation with almost sinful empathy: "I bet you don't know what's going on here at Buffalo, do you?" I allowed that I didn't, and he continued with exuberant virtuosity, portraying an academic New Jerusalem of "unlimited money, a $650,000,000 new campus, bold and new organizational ideas, President Meyerson, the number of new faculty and administrators to be added, the romance of taking a mediocre up-state university and creating—well—*the Berkeley of the East.*" I was totally captivated by his Utopian rhapsody. Even his New Frontier jargon didn't put me off, although Touster blushes now when I revive his memories of the "very first telephone call," when he referred to Meyerson as a "Kennedy type," himself as "McGeorge Bundy," and Meyerson's predecessor, Clifford C. Furnas, as "Eisenhower."

I was smitten by Saul Touster, his verve, his *chutzpah,* his ability to evoke shades of an academic Eden. I was put off only by his "Berkeley of the East" routine. The Avis syndrome, "No. 2 but trying harder," afflicts many universities. Mimicking charismatic institutions in their twilight is no way to build a great university. But the Avis syndrome is deeply embedded. I heard recently that the University of California at Santa Cruz is being touted as the "Buffalo of the West," while the University of Maryland claims to be the "Santa Cruz of the East."

Until Touster approached me, the University of Buffalo was a largely unknown quantity to me. I knew that it was the principal upstate campus of the New York State University system and that earlier it had been a private university whose medical school in particular had earned some distinction. I remember calling David Riesman at Harvard in early March of 1967 to ask him what he thought of Buffalo. He had taught at its Law School in the late 1930s and was now advising President Meyerson on social science matters. Riesman was generally optimistic. He compared Buffalo's academic qualities to marble cake: "Some departments awfully soggy and depressed; others fluffy and rising." Riesman had lived in nearby Canada while teaching at UB. In the days before eco-awareness, he found the view of industrial Buffalo from across Lake Ontario "aesthetically fetching—especially the chartreuse and black and mauve smoke against the steel-gray sky."

Looking into the Buffalo situation closely, I discovered that there was indeed reason for optimism. Buffalo was clearly on the move. Less than five years before, the private University of Buffalo had merged with the public state university system as the campus' one hope for financial solvency. At that time Meyerson's predecessor, Clifford Furnas, had fought courageously to ensure the campus a high degree of autonomy in spite of its affiliation with the state. Furnas was determined that UB would not be, in his own homely term, "a numbered restaurant in a Howard Johnson chain." That remark and others like it (including an outspoken interview with Fred Hechinger in the education section of the *Times*) permanently alienated Furnas from the state university central administration in Albany and ultimately cost him the option of delaying his retirement by several years. His successful negotiation of the merger was the outstanding achievement of the Furnas years at Buffalo. In the four years following the merger Buffalo steadily expanded on many fronts, from hiring a number of outstanding faculty (including novelist John Barth and critic Leslie Fiedler) to preliminary planning for a multimillion dollar new campus. When Furnas retired in 1966, a committee of forward-looking faculty hit on Meyerson as the successor best suited to realize the enormous potential implicit in UB's emergence as a major graduate center in the state university system.

During my first visit to Buffalo, on February 8, 1967, I met with the department chairmen and deans of the social sciences and administration faculty. These fifteen or so men represented some 350 faculty members within the area of the university that I was being asked to lead as provost. Lunch was cordial enough. On my right was Professor Daniel Hamberg, chairman of the department of economics, who bragged playfully about taking a second-rate department and building it into a good one via panzer-like raids on other universities. He was especially proud of "a fabulous package deal" (literally fabulous, it turned out) to recruit eight recent MIT Ph.D.s en bloc. On my left was Professor Albert Somit, chairman of the political science department, who told me that UB had had no political science department until three years before. The department now numbered twenty-seven and in the next five years would be enlarged to forty-five faculty. Other growth promises were formidable. The Buffalo campus was going to be the "jewel in the state university crown," promising to double its student body and professoriat in the next five years' time. This depended, I also learned, on the building of the enormous new campus. When I asked the projected completion date of the new campus, everybody suddenly got very busy with his food—except Saul Touster, better in person even than on the phone. Throughout the meeting, Touster had simultaneously played the parts of MC, interlocutor, moderator, censor, and press agent. Zero Mostel on speed. Touster assured me over the rising clatter of knives and forks that the new campus would go up on schedule. "Figure on five years or so," he said.

Before I could continue this line of questioning, Touster shuttled us to a nearby conference room where, according to my schedule, we were to have a two-hour conference. Touster left for another appointment, to my despair, because it soon became clear that no one knew what the assembled group was supposed to do together for two hours. Absentmindedly I took a place at the head of a long table, then realized it might seem presumptuous, but sat on uncomfortably where I was—very alone and facing rows of empty chairs. Two or three of the group sat away from the table, by the door near the back of the room. A dozen others were clustered at the *very* bottom of the bowling-alley-length table, like tenpins, I thought.

After fifteen minutes or so, I cleared my throat and said, "Maybe we ought to start the meeting." The tenpins nodded, and the group by the door stopped talking and looked my way. But I didn't know where to go from there, and neither did they. There was more silence. Finally, Hamberg, the economics chairman, raised his hand. "Professor Bennis, what do you think the function of provost is?" he asked. I told him I would like that question answered too, since the provost structure had not been explained to me. "I wonder if you could tell me what you *think* the functions of the provost are?" Hamberg would have none of this table-turning; and now, in an Alphonse-Gaston act that must have lasted ten minutes, we lobbed the question back and forth. "You most certainly did not come to Buffalo without any awareness of the role for which you are now being interviewed?" he said. In fact, I did come to Buffalo with only the fuzziest awareness, since Meyerson and Touster had been long on enthusiasm and very short on such administrative specifics as precise responsibilities. So I said again that I knew little about it and would prefer to hear from them first. Then, I promised rather archly, I would respond. Hamberg and I had reached one of those strange impasses that occur sometimes in interviews. Aside from genuine vagueness about the role, I had a sense that what the group most wanted was a skeet to shoot at, and somehow or other I did not want to give them a target. Hamberg and I continued to wrestle politely, the grunts practically audible in the quiet conference room.

During the encounter, several mentioned Meyerson's interest

in "superstars" and "glamor" appointments—glamor being defined,
I learned, as a Harvard A.B., an Oxford doctorate, and a BBC
accent. There were also chortles about the Frank Lloyd Wright
house, purchased by the state for $65,000, which the Meyersons
planned to move into.

The interview could not have been much fun for those
conducting it. Interviewing potential bosses never is. Besides, in the
tussle with Hamberg, I had broken the rule that the candidate
gamely answers the question, whatever it is. The interviewers, no
doubt, saw me as Meyerson's choice for the job. There was no mis-
taking an undercurrent of hostility, and I felt that the faculty leaders resented having to participate in what they saw less as an honest,
open-ended interview than a formality to be followed by a rubber
stamp.

I felt that the deans and chairmen there were generally
honest—honest and scared, and probably with good reason. At one
of Meyerson's first press conferences as UB president, he was reported to have wondered if the department chairmen would prove
big enough men to be capable of hiring people better than they
themselves were, a remarkable opener for a new president presumably trying to gain the confidence and support of his faculty. Several
questioned me closely about my relationship with Meyerson; some-
body even asked whether we were cousins, mentioning a current
rumor to that effect. I said I had not yet even *met* Meyerson, was
supposed to meet him that morning at the airport on his way to
New York, but that my plane had arrived too late.

Driving me back to the airport that evening, Saul Touster
went only slightly out of his way to show me still another tantaliz-
ing Frank Lloyd Wright house, supposedly for sale not far from
Meyerson's. The house, I later learned, had already been sold to
another recruit, Karl Willenbrock, the new provost of engineering
and applied science. We swung by the Riesman-admired smoke-
stacks along the lake for a romantic finale. As we drove, Touster
began a new and puzzling line of questioning on my work at MIT
as department chairman, particularly my consulting activities for the
Department of State, ALCAN, and other industrial organizations.
(Over a year later, in May 1968 at a goodbye party for Touster as
he left Buffalo for another assignment, I asked him about those

puzzling questions. He told me that a number of faculty members had wondered whether my connection with the "military-industrial complex" and my management-school background were compatible with the liberal educational goals of Buffalo.) The interview that afternoon and the puzzling questions aside, I felt good about the day. One reason was Touster himself. A formidably intelligent, complicated man, Touster had not only charmed me, he had also deeply impressed me with the humaneness of his idea of a university. Whether I go to Buffalo or not, I told Clurie when I arrived home, I've made a friend.

I met Martin Meyerson about a week later, on February 16, 1967 at our house on Beacon Hill. That meeting lasted three hours. I had heard a good deal about Meyerson before, all positive, from Cambridge sources. Meyerson was thought to be unusually well prepared for the kind of turmoil afflicting almost all large universities. From 1959 to 1963 he was the first director of the Harvard-MIT Joint Center for Urban Studies (somewhat overshadowed by his subsequent successor, Daniel Moynihan); he then went to Berkeley as dean of the college of environmental design; as acting chancellor at Berkeley, he administered to the reassembled wreckage after the student upheavals of 1965. Before initiating the joint center, he had been a student in classics at Columbia and had established himself as a leading scholar of urban planning, teaching at Chicago and then at Pennsylvania.

To be with Meyerson was a pleasure. His mind and imagination ranged, both historically and comparatively, over the widest variety of topics. He seemed to know almost everybody. He could think of nine things at once, always with a beautiful anecdote and a conceptual grasp. As a recruiter, Meyerson's ace in the hole was a truly monumental plan for redesigning Buffalo's conventional departments-schools-and-colleges academic structure. His plan had been ratified by the UB faculty senate only two months after his arrival at Buffalo in November 1966. As Meyerson summarized his academic plan for me, the university was undergoing the following changes:

(1) The ninety some existing departments were to be restructured into seven new faculties, each with a provost as the chief

academic and administrative officer. The provosts would be selected for their academic eminence, broad scholarship, and administrative ability. Each faculty would consist of the basic disciplines within the newly defined area plus relevant professional schools. The faculty he wanted me to head would be composed of all the basic social science disciplines, from anthropology to psychology, and also (to the chagrin of the arts and letters provost) philosophy and history as well as the faculty of the schools of management and social welfare. Interdisciplinary programs would be encouraged, and the provost would have ample resources and administrative leeway to implement new education ventures.

(2) Augmenting and complementing the seven-faculty structure, thirty new colleges, small enough to be intellectual communities, would be built on the new campus, each housing only four hundred students with up to six hundred more commmuting students as affiliates. These colleges would serve residential, social, and educational functions. Faculty and students would live and work together in the meaningful human relationships of these "intellectual neighborhoods." Meyerson, who had only recently come from the archetypical multiversity, saw the smaller colleges as a way to offset the apathy and anomie characteristic of an enormous campus. A secondary purpose was to counteract the stranglehold that traditional departments have on the typical university. The colleges would provide a truly educational experience, not just a narrow academic one, particularly for undergraduates, who too often receive only a watered-down version of what professors teach to their graduate students. I thought this idea stunning. It would develop closer faculty-student relationships while providing the best of two possible worlds: the complex diversity of a large university, the communal advantages of smaller "living and learning" units.

(3) University-wide action-research centers or councils on international studies, urban studies, and higher educational studies would act as magnets for scholars and students drawn from the entire university (and outside) to work together on such vital central issues.

I was impressed with Meyerson's overall concept. Several aspects of the plan were especially attractive to me: the decentralization of authority; the development of a multicircuited university with many different focuses of collegiality (if you didn't find the right fit in a department, there was always a college or a center to connect up with); a conviction that administrators should be scholars and that a five-year period was about the optimum number of years one should stay in an administrative capacity before returning to one's scholarship. I was also impressed with Meyerson's clear intent to raise the self-esteem of the university, the self-esteem of the faculty and students, and also the self-esteem of the general Buffalo community—a big working-class population, predominantly Polish in derivation, in a city that is the butt of numberless bad jokes like those that plague less vulnerable Philadelphia.

Meyerson also assured me that with the new campus sufficient resources would be available to build quality on top of the university's inevitable deadwood, the less competent holdovers from previous administrations. By going easy on the University's former power structure, we could avoid a collision course with "old UB." I would also have the resources, and his support, he assured me, for an experimental Ph.D. program that I hoped to develop in the applied social sciences.

When I questioned Meyerson about the political climate of New York State, mindful of Governor Ronald Reagan's campaign against the University of California system, he replied confidently, "Well, Warren, if you compare the former governors of California with those of New York, you can see the difference: Roosevelt, Smith, Lehman, Harriman, Rockefeller . . ."

As we became more at ease with each other, I asked him what his own goal for Buffalo was. He paused for at least thirty seconds and answered: "To make it a university where I would like to stay and be a professor after finishing my administrative responsibilities." When my wife, Clurie, joined us, she asked him what the city of Buffalo offered, say, compared with Boston. The pause that followed grew into a long silence. Finally Meyerson's face brightened. "It's more comprehensible," he said.

I was sold on the man and his conceptual vision. Meyerson's gift as a recruiter was his ability to transmogrify all the highly visible drawbacks of Buffalo and make them reappear in the guise of exhilarating challenges. I knew after those mesmerizing three hours that if he asked me to join this twentieth-century Republic of

Virtue, I would accept. The timing seemed perfect; Meyerson's
new organizational design would go into effect on the same day as
my term of office, September 1, 1967.

Colleagues at the Sloan School of Management, one of the
five schools at MIT, were unsympathetic when I announced that I
was considering an offer to be provost at Buffalo. Their attitude toward all administrative jobs in the university—any university—
bordered on contempt. "God," said one, "why do you want to
waste your time shuffling papers?" Then gales of laughter following
a crack about snow-blowers being a fantastic growth industry.

I was frankly in conflict about leaving the Boston-Cambridge
area. At MIT I enjoyed the comfortable life of a full professor, a
life which included lucrative opportunities for consulting, terrifyingly
bright students, and excellent colleagues. I had written my clutch
of books and had established some repute as an organizational
theorist. MIT was paradise for an organizational theorist. It
attracted a steady stream of practicing executives who came to the
Boston area to acquire advanced degrees in management. For over
a decade they were the human crucible in which I was able to test
new hypotheses, new approaches. But after ten years the insulated
atmosphere of MIT was becoming a little too comfortable, too predictable. I was hungry for practical experience of my own. The
provostship at Buffalo might be just the opportunity I wanted to
apply social science theory from a position of authority in a complex academic organization.

During the next six weeks, I went through an acutely irreso-
lute, Hamletic phase. My decision-making wasn't helped by the
fact that after Clurie and I had flown to Buffalo for her first trip
and my second she had a miscarriage. She spent the next month
mostly in bed. Even for a recruiting trip, that late winter visit to
Buffalo was unusually unpleasant. Being scrutinized every waking
minute is exhausting anyway, and the flight took four hours, late
each way. And, God, was it cold. As I walked down the roll-away
stairs into the white swirl of the Buffalo International runway, I
wondered whether it was true, what a disgruntled native son had
told me, that summer in Buffalo was three weeks of bad ice-skating.

Before a firm offer came, there were several mildly dis-
tressing signals at odds with the utopian view of Buffalo that Meyer-

son had painted. First, Saul Touster asked me to return to the campus at once. He explained that Meyerson and he were getting flak from certain members of the social sciences faculty in regard to my likely appointment. Apparently, no formal search committee had been set up, and the faculty were now demanding one. Some faculty spokesmen, "with nothing against you personally," Touster assured me, insisted on a formal procedure. I told Saul that I thought I had gone through that already. He answered that generally he was in charge of recruiting provosts and other top administrators. I had assumed that the previous informal procedure with the consultation was adequate, but this time the faculty were pressing for another look. "People are paranoid," he said. I thought I understood.[1]

I also learned that the building plans were not firm but vague and uncertain. Actually, the $650,000,000 figure mentioned during my interview had only once been cited by Governor Rockefeller. The only place it currently appeared in writing was in a *Time* article quoting Meyerson. Furthermore, a major controversy was raging in Buffalo over where the new campus should be located. Three different sites were being advocated: a characterless 1,200-acre suburban tract (where, at this writing, construction of the campus has finally begun), a downtown site, and expansion of the existing 178-acre campus onto an adjacent public golf course. When news of the campus controversy reached me in Cambridge, I was unpleasantly surprised. Meyerson had never said so, but for some

[1] Barbara Probst Solomon, who taught during 1967–68 in Buffalo's English department, wrote in an article "Life in the Yellow Submarine: Buffalo's SUNY" (*Harper's*, 1968, *237*, p. 98): "I've always been fond of paranoia as a life style, but paranoia on a grand scale, preferably in some major European capital with good restaurants to plot in. Of course, for paranoia to work, I've always believed you have to have a lot of spare time; with the new small teaching loads (average of two courses a week), the placing of sixty-five assorted geniuses, poets, writers (Lionel Abel, Robert Creeley, John Logan, Leslie Fiedler, John Barth among them), the scholars looking nervously at writers, writers feeling sullen among all those Ph.D. types, all crammed together in a cinder-block Stalag 17 office, additionally huddled together because the university has no connection with the town of Buffalo—and even more intensely huddled together because the Life of the Mind is being carried on in brutal weather and with an ugliness of surroundings that took imagination to produce—one is often overwhelmed by the sheer weight of the paranoia."

reason I had fantasied an academic Mont-Saint-Michel already
substantially existent on the plains of western New York.

Momentary qualms aside, Meyerson and his vision of Buffalo
excited me, and I knew that I had wanted to go there almost from
the moment Saul Touster first phoned. Notorious weather, paranoia, uncertainty about the building plans, chartreuse industrial
smoke, even the thought of life in the provinces—none of these
seriously lessened my enthusiasm.

After Touster had assuaged the social sciences faculty,
Meyerson made a firm offer. By then I also had offers from two
schools in Southern California. Winter was nearly over in Boston.
While I weighed alternatives and juggled possible career choices,
real life intruded one morning when I discovered that our vestibule
had been broken into and all the family's winter coats stolen. The
bad weather lifted that day. Drawn outside by the spring air, I took
a pleasant stroll over to Filene's basement and mindlessly purchased
a new overcoat—the heaviest alpaca snowcoat in the entire store.

In late March I gave Meyerson my answer: "Yes."

Largely under the spell of Meyerson's bold dreams and
blandishments, others also made the pilgrimage to Buffalo. Two
other provost designees accepted at about the same time I did. Eric
Larrabee, a suave and brilliant New York editor (*Harper's, Hori-
zon*), became provost of arts and letters, and Karl Willenbrock, as
mentioned earlier, agreed to leave his post as associate dean of
applied sciences at Harvard after twenty years to head Buffalo's
engineering faculty. The four remaining provosts called for in the
reorganization plan were recruited from faculty already at UB.

Larrabee, Willenbrock, and I—Meyerson's three chief outside recruits—arrived on campus that fall with all the confidence
and optimism of young princes joining a crusade. Only Willenbrock
had had first-hand experience in educational administration above
the chairman level, but our inexperience didn't deter us in the least.
It only served to make us more confident, more optimistic. In this
academic great good place, creativity would count for more than
narrowly defined training and credentials.

We were Meyerson's champions in this cause, and we looked
the part. I remember the entrance we made at the first provosts'
meeting. Karl Willenbrock, who had snatched that other Wright-

designed house, invited me to it for breakfast before the meeting. Afterward, as Karl and I climbed into his white Porsche convertible, his wife, Millie, came out to wave goodbye and handed us berets to protect us from the wind. We drove from Willenbrock's Wright house to Larrabee's Wright house (formerly an adjunct to Meyerson's Wright house). Eric was waiting for us with homburg erectly perched and umbrella furled. So caparisoned in homburg and berets, the three of us drove in rising euphoria under the warm September sun onto the small, tree-covered campus. We felt that we epitomized Buffalo's new look. Style was the byword. Whether we succeeded in making Buffalo great, we were confident we would give it style.

"Style" was the magic word that year at Buffalo, one rich with associations with the Kennedy years. Meyerson's urbanity and grace inevitably led to comparisons with John Kennedy's. We outside recruits were Meyerson's New Frontiersmen, and some did feel, clinging to Buffalo's few cultural amenities (notably the Albright-Knox Art Gallery and the Buffalo Philharmonic), as if we were laboring on the extreme edges of the civilized world. Happily, such snobbism was only a minor characteristic of the Meyerson new look. Mostly it consisted of a breathtaking optimism. State University of New York was going to become a new, better California system.

Meyerson brought a subtlety to the institution's hunger for greatness. He eschewed the heavy-handed "Boost Buffalo" approach of his predecessors, but he was no less attuned than folksy Cliff Furnas had been to the necessity of image-building. From the start Meyerson had an enviable national press. His ideas turned up regularly in the education sections of *Time* and *Newsweek*. On campus he began a systematic attack on the aura of provincialism that still clung to UB. Making the Frank Lloyd Wright house the president's new residence was part of it. Designating his new layer of administrators "provosts" was another. Besides a general uncertainty about the proper pronunciation of the word, there was speculation about what a provost could do that a dean or vice president could not. In fact, the distinction was real. Meyerson conceived of the provosts as senior *academic* officers, who would be sensitive to the needs of individual faculty and important educational goals and not simply responsive to organizational requirements. For example, the dean of the college of arts and sciences was replaced by several provosts, each representing a natural family of related disciplines (arts and letters, for example). The idea was simple and admirable, even if the title was a bit pretentious.

Meyerson's taste is extraordinary, and his campaign to change UB's image was remarkably successful. No aspect of university life was unaffected. At one point the university retained the services of graphic designers Chermayeff & Geismar Associates to advise on ways to express UB's new look visually. At a rumored fee of ten thousand dollars, Ivan Chermayeff himself was charged with designing a new logo for the university to replace the clutter and conventional academic symbolism of the old one. The new seal was to appear on everything from catalogs to garbage cans (the latter proved impractical). More than a million pieces of stationery with the new seal were printed up. That changeover took a year of hassling with the state over the grade of paper, a specially mixed ink, and a nonstandard typeface, all specified by the designer in blissful ignorance of state purchasing procedures.

The climax of the image-building effort was the new president's inauguration in late May 1967. Among the forty-two dignitaries on the platform with Meyerson were educational superstars Clark Kerr, a former colleague from the Berkeley of the West, and Yale's charismatic President Brewster. On an enormous silver screen behind the platform party flashed the larger-than-life image of Governor Nelson Rockefeller, adding his good wishes for the occasion via the medium of sound on film. The theme of Meyerson's inaugural address was the realization of greatness through implementation of the letter and spirit of the academic reorganization. "If we have the courage to be different, we shall not long be different because the model of State University of New York at Buffalo will become a model for many."

Rain forced the inaugural luncheon indoors. When the skies cleared, the guests moved on to the new president's new house for a reception. The Meyersons shook 1,500 hands as guests lined up across the lawn and down the driveway, at one point waiting in the reception line for as long as forty-five minutes. Shuttle busses ran every ten minutes from the parking lot of the nearby Buffalo zoo, where guests had been requested to leave their cars. Once through the line, the guests explored the house itself, a rambling, low-ceilinged gem that Buffalo had ignored for the half century since Wright completed it. The house was almost devoid of furniture. But even bare and unrestored it was a dramatic backdrop for the final moments of a pageant unlike any in the university's first 120 years.

Now that a changed economy has radically altered our perceptions, the Meyerson inauguration seems almost frivolous. But at the time it was simply the least important manifestation of a pervasive commitment to change. Buffalo desperately needed new blood. Meyerson and his men were transfusing her.

My first year as social sciences provost was marked by an impressive list of "transitions," to borrow *Newsweek*'s unemotional term. During 1967–68, I recruited nine new chairmen and two deans for the faculty, changing about 90 per cent of the leadership personnel of the social sciences area. The faculty also gained forty-five new full-time faculty members that year (a net increase of thirty, owing to a number of departures). Almost three fourths of my time that first year was spent recruiting. I interviewed over three hundred candidates.

Buffalo raided from Harvard, Yale, and Princeton. Each new appointment meant an exponential increase in enthusiasm, new ideas, the Meyerson optimism. The tiny crowded campus barely seemed able to contain all the excitement within it. Intellectual neighborhoods sprang up across the campus, each dominated by the personality of a "new look" appointee. Lawrence Chisolm inaugurated a radical American studies program that emphasized the study of non-American cultures as a way of overcoming chauvinistic biases. David Hays inherited a good but narrowly defined linguistics program and made it magnetic by insisting that linguistics was no less than a focus for intellectual integration. John Eberhard, the new dean of architecture and environmental design, attracted a nucleus of nonestablishment designers interested in creating living systems rather than monuments. To head a new library school, a dean with an applied math background was hired. He shocked an assembly of catalogers by asking who exactly Melville (Dewey Decimal System) Dewey *was* and then proceeded to attract to the school a flock of media freaks, sensitivity trainers, and, less unusual for a library school, systems specialists. The new social welfare dean, Franklin Zweig, young enough to be called "boy dean" by his detractors, turned the social work school upside down. Social work at Buffalo was no longer to be the handmaiden of psychiatry. Under Zweig, the emphasis would be on community organization, legal and social policy. Richard Brandenburg, new dean of the school of management, also broadened the scope of the management school to include public institutions. Changes were seen in the least likely places. For example, Leroy Pesch, who came from Stanford to head the medical school, took steps toward streamlining the medical curriculum. Talk at the medical school was somewhat less of the narrow professional concerns of private practice and more of the health-care needs of the public.

The change was pervasive. Almost 75 per cent of the present Buffalo faculty were appointed under Meyerson. The newcomers were largely a self-selected group, committed to innovation and risk-taking. The student body was also changing. By 1968, 80 per cent of the entering freshmen were in the top tenth of their high school graduating classes, compared to only 10 per cent ten years before. This upward trend in the quality of Buffalo's undergraduates had begun when the campus affiliated with the state university. Going State had resulted in an influx of bright applicants from the New York City area. Along with Stony Brook on Long Island, Buffalo was regarded as one of the state university's radical campuses, which left some people wondering whether Meyerson's Berkeley of the East approach may have had an appeal that he had not fully calculated.

For that one year, 1967–68, Buffalo was an academic Camelot. The provosts met around the president's conference table ready to work miracles. Signals occasionally reached me that not everyone on campus took us quite as seriously as we did ourselves. On my coat rack one morning I found that someone had hung a Batman cape. The anonymous critic had a point. The atmosphere in Hayes Hall was a bit heavy with omnipotent fantasy.

Although living quarters on the new campus were still in the future, six "human-sized" colleges got underway at once. Meyerson named a master for each of them. Almost immediately these colleges provoked controversy. Meyerson wanted innovation, yes, but rumors began to circulate that course cards for College A (the six colleges were referred to by initials until formal applications for names were approved) were being sold, snatched up by students who intended to do little or nothing and reward themselves with A's at the end of the semester. "Why do you think they call it College A?" one cynical student asked. There were tales of credit being given for trips to Europe and building bird cages.

The master of College A regarded any impugning of its grading system as an antirevolutionary tactic. No one in the Meyerson administration, including myself, wanted to take a harsh public stand against this nonsense, particularly after College A and its master had become the target of community attack. Foolishly, we let the more change-resistant "old faculty" appropriate to themselves the role of guardians of academic standards.

There were other rumblings in paradise. The centers were not doing well. It was easier to break down barriers than build bridges, we learned. The center for higher education, for example, did not generate new programs or attract faculty and students, as planned. Since Meyerson had never made explicit the goals or functions of the center, its newly appointed head dissipated much of his energy in writing voluminous memos requesting more direction. The center for international studies had existed prior to the reorganization and did function, but not much more effectively than before. More paper, in the form of a newsletter, was the only substantial sign of its new status. The center for urban studies was undertaking a series of much-needed but thoroughly conventional projects in Buffalo's inner city.

In one form or another all the faculties had their problems. Many departments resisted the new faculty structure. I sometimes felt that our many individual accomplishments, a promising new program, the appointment of a particularly good teacher or administrator, somehow did not add up to a significantly changed

university; that somehow our gains were not being consolidated
and might somehow slip away. These concerns prompted me to
write in my provost's report for 1967–68:

> Each of [the university's] virtues could be transformed over-
> night into obstacles and problems. Spectacular growth could lead
> to a "change for change sake" mentality, culminating in a mas-
> sive and mediocre institution; the new university organization
> with its seven faculties, three university-wide deans, seven uni-
> versity vice presidents, three councils, thirty colleges (and what
> have I forgotten?) could become a wild Night at the Opera with
> the Marx Brothers; and tax-based universities are vulnerable to
> the biennial vicissitudes and vagaries of intramural politics.

But such moments of doubt were rare.

In August 1968, Meyerson asked me to step up from social
sciences provost to be the university's vice-president for academic
affairs. The official press release on my appointment said that my
responsibilities included coordination of educational programs,
working in the development of educational innovations and policies,
and special responsibility for the colleges and the university's communication resources. One surprising consequence was that I was
suddenly very much in demand in the Buffalo community. Shortly
after the announcement, a group of citizens even asked me to consider running for mayor. "On what ticket?" I asked. "It doesn't
matter."

Camelot lasted barely a thousand days.

7

What Went Wrong

"*Y*ou know, I never asked you about this, Warren, but do you ever feel guilty about bringing me to Buffalo?"

Theodore Mills, who had left Yale to head Buffalo's sociology department, had dropped in to say goodbye the weekend before Clurie and I moved to Cincinnati. Mills had had a rough time at Buffalo: responsibility for the campus's most politicized, most polarized department; a scathing public attack in the campus paper; constant run-ins with the new university administration. Since then he has resigned as chairman; but for some time after I had decided to leave, he was still holding on. He laughed as he asked how I felt. *He* clearly was angry.

I thought about the question for a minute. I did feel guilty. "Yes," I said.

"Well, you should."

If they were as frank as Mills, many would probably tell Meyerson and me the same thing. They rode into Buffalo on the crest of our enthusiasm. More than four years later, the campus mood is dismal.

I had gone to Buffalo seeking Camelot. Camelot's shining moment was brief indeed.

Three years after my arrival, Buffalo was a different university:

Chancellor Gould and President Meyerson had both departed, as had Peter Regan.

Karl Willenbrock resigned in December 1970, to take a post with the National Bureau of Standards.

Eric Larrabee resigned that same summer to head the New York State Council of the Arts. (A prominent member of the SUNY trustees and fundraiser for the Republican Party tried to sabotage his appointment by Rockefeller simply because Larrabee was associated with the "permissive Meyerson regime.")

The six colleges were struggling for their existence, the initial energies and ideas behind them dissipated.

All directors of the three special centers or councils had resigned, and only one center, that for international studies, was still in operation.

Ground was broken on the new campus in suburban Amherst, New York, by Governor Rockefeller on Halloween Day, 1968. The governor reported to the press that he "struck water with the first shovel." Actual construction got underway in September 1970. The delay, coupled with the extraordinary inflation of the last several years, will result in construction of a much more spartan campus than originally proposed.

Practically every appointment made by Meyerson and most of the other "Meyerson men" was turned into a resignation or a termination by the new administration headed by Robert Ketter.

One of the original provosts still held his job. One of the last holdouts was my successor as social sciences provost, who was there during the pre-Meyersonian days. The undergraduate dean appointed by Meyerson (a distinguished political scientist then not yet thirty, trained at Harvard and Oxford) was also forced to resign as dean.

The great majority of officials appointed by the new Ketter administration had been at Buffalo for most of their academic lives, predating, in some cases, the Eisenhower years and the tenure of

Clifford Furnas. The new provost of the health sciences (now called vice president for health affairs), for example, was sixty-six and had been at the UB school of medicine for thirty-three years.

Several superstars had left. Education critic Edgar Z. Friedenberg had gone to Nova Scotia; C. H. Waddington, the biologist and futurist who held the university's lucrative Einstein chair, had returned prematurely to Britain. Radical historian Gabriel Kolko had gone to York University in Toronto. There was no stampede from the university (Nobel Prize–winning physiologist Sir John Eccles remains), but a steady, outward trickle, unhappily coupled with a state university-wide moratorium on hiring.

Even the Frank Lloyd Wright houses had lost their identification with the university. Karl Willenbrock sold his to an outsider. The Larrabees retained their house, but are no longer affiliated with the university. President Ketter left the Wright house that Meyerson had chosen, claiming publicly that the roof leaked and privately that the ceiling was "too damn low" for his 6′+. Instead he moved into a residence purchased by the UB Foundation at a cost of $125,000. The Wright house now houses the UB alumni office and the university archives, coupled, for all anyone can determine, only because of their alphabetical proximity.

Much more serious than change in specific personnel was the shifting mood at the university. The atmosphere was one of diminished expectations. To some extent this was a national problem, the function of the recession and great war weariness. But it was more than that. The many faculty who came to Buffalo during Meyerson's brief tenure were understandably unhappy with the conservative administration that replaced him. But the discontent went deeper and was more widespread than that.

Even moderate and conservative faculty were concerned about the malaise that prevailed on campus. As philosophy professor Paul Kurtz wrote in May 1971 in the university paper, the *Reporter:*

> Many faculty within this university now believe . . . that the overriding problem that we now face concerns the apparent *decline in the level of academic aspirations* of the State University of New York at Buffalo. At least there is the widespread impression that the present administration is doing very little to raise our

goals. Indeed, it now seems that the vision of a great university
that so stirred SUNYAB from the day it went State until 1970 has
been seriously narrowed and restricted.

Although many faculty members were critical of President
Meyerson's administration, nevertheless his administration demonstrated a concern for stature and it promised greatness. It was
motivated by a desire to reach a high level of achievement. One
can only regret that this forward-looking leadership has been
largely absent in the first year of this new administration. All sec-
tors of the university, the right and the left, the students and
faculty now sense the mood of second best that seems to prevail.

From 1962 through 1970 SUNYAB attracted a great number of distinguished scholars, many of them world-renowned. As
far as we can tell, there have been few, if any, distinguished appointments made this past year. Indeed, a number of excellent
scholars have resigned from the university, some of them because
of the general impression that UB has passed its moment of greatness and is entering a period of decline. Many younger colleagues
are exasperated by the recent defense of a quota system for tenure
and promotions, which is primarily based upon grounds of economy rather than academic excellence.

The administration should be committed to the building
of a *great* university—the leading graduate center in the state
university. I am not thinking simply in quantitative fiscal terms
but in *qualitative* terms. And I am thinking of the need to develop
bold educational programs fused with solid academic criteria. As
far as I can tell, very few, if any, educational innovations have
been suggested or introduced by this administration.

That analysis was made by one of the more conservative
members of the faculty (a man who describes himself as Old Left,
lest by conservative I suggest the Goldwater breed). The liberal and
radical faculty feel even greater alienation. As the master of one
of the colleges wrote to me:

> I do not see the colleges as capable of steady growth and
> persistence. I fear that what we are going to get from the new
> administration are arguments about scarce resources that are
> really policy arguments in disguise, and that the tendency of
> policy will be to squeeze the colleges bit by bit into difficulty—
> not assault or abolish them. . . . It's hard to see the future as
> even modestly rosy for the efforts now underway.

So it is a peculiar time. People are working more on matters of direct and personal interest to them, in contrast to the

highly political and public year just passed, but this is not the same as a return to academic privatization. Lots of good things are going on, while at the same time the general picture of possibilities—within the university—looks bleaker. An essay in the Whole Earth Catalogue recently was entitled, Think Little. That's where we are.

The diminution of spirit at the university is the result of many factors. The narrower ambition of the current administration is one, a very important one. But another, unfortunately, was the failure of the former administration to deliver a package to match the promise.

Whether anyone could have turned UB into a permanent academic Utopia in three short years is doubtful. But the warning signals of weaknesses that would ultimately prove fatal were there early in the attempt, and we in the Meyerson administration consistently ignored them. In the euphoria of the place we paid little attention to valuable, objective intelligence we occasionally received from the outside. For example, in late November 1968 the campus was visited by Dr. Dwight Ladd, representing the Carnegie Commission on the Future of Higher Education. Ladd's report, summarized and distributed by the then-director of UB's center of higher education, Edward Joseph Shoben, was uncanny in its perception of the precise areas that subsequently emerged as pitfalls. Had Buffalo changed, Ladd wondered, or had it experienced only the illusion of change? As Shoben summed up:

> Has anything fundamental happened at SUNY-Buffalo, or has only a brilliantly conceived and handsomely engineered superstructure been built over a pretty conventional hull? Except for some of our programs for the disadvantaged, which have evoked both large enthusiasm and critical opposition, he found our reorganization still the big topic for discussion. For Ladd, this fact of local life has an ominous quality. The reorganization is visible, dramatic, massive—and without necessary impact on individual faculty members. In short, it permits people to live in both worlds, that of superficially exciting change and that of actually comfortable academic conventionality. Although the individual professor is free to talk about it with interest and even pride, he is not required by our new organizational patterns to alter his outlook or his professional conduct in any special fashion.

As a corollary, Ladd noticed that many educationally conservative faculty remained in informal positions of influence. He
predicted that, if directly challenged, these individuals would exert
a considerable force against the pattern of change created by Meyerson. The events following Meyerson's decision to go to Pennsylvania
proved Ladd absolutely right. Conservative faculty capitalized on
anti-Meyersonian feeling in the Buffalo community, exacerbated
by the violence of the student strike, and succeeded in catapulting
their own candidate to the university presidency.

The Meyerson administration had been insensitive to the
hurtfulness of status deprivation. The old guard were frequently
overlooked at such nonacademic but important prestige-building
functions as presidential dinner parties for visiting dignitaries.
Clifford Furnas may have been short on style, but he knew how to
use a committee assignment or a seat in the president's box at a
football game to make an ally. Meyerson brought supporters with
him. He didn't make many new ones.

Ladd also spotted the extent to which the academic reorganization had complicated the university's already baroque structure.
"Repeatedly," Shoben wrote, "people asked whether we were en-
tangling ourselves in a plurality of agencies [faculties, colleges,
schools, councils, programs, departments, and workshops, to name
only the major units] that define less of an administrative foliage
while other and more usual [basic] . . . interests became lost in
the unnecessarily created forest."[1] Many individuals, even those in
general harmony with Meyerson's goals, felt that the reorganization
did little more than add an extra layer to the administration. The
addition of provosts with their associates and assistants and staffs
to the existing hierarchy of deans and vice presidents did swell the
university bureaucracy to a remarkable degree. This administrative
redundancy has become an argument for the present administration's plan for yet another academic reorganization. The Ketter
proposal would streamline the administration somewhat, but it
might also result in stamping out the last vestiges of the Meyerson
spirit. No one is sanguine at the prospect of the institution's being

[1] Personal communication from writer.

completely overhauled every three years as the first order of business
of each new administration. The human cost of that would be
frightful.

Perhaps if Meyerson had stayed, if there had been no
campus strike in 1970, if a less conventional administration had
followed, if the money had held out, things would be different. But
Buffalo is no longer the academic new frontier. As a major university in the New York State system, it isn't Podunk either. But
the pervasive excitement of 1968 and 1969 is gone. Now one finds
it only in isolated programs, with individual faculty and students.
The law school, for example, provides humane professional education, is innovative and unorthodox, has become a model for law
schools throughout the nation. The English department still thrives.
There are some others as well that remind one of the former spirit.
But for me and many others who left, the Buffalo experience is
irretrievably over. I look back on it now with enormous nostalgia.
As an educational experiment the Meyerson years at Buffalo were
not a major success. No permanent change in the nation's expectations for higher education can be identified with our attempt to
radically transform the University. What does remain is a nucleus
of people who form an informal Buffalo group, in much the same
way one thinks of individuals identified with the University of
Chicago or Black Mountain College as a group. All of us were
deeply touched by the Buffalo experience. For a time Buffalo was
the locus of enormous excitement, as great as any we had experienced in our academic careers. Hopes and ambitions were high.
For a time Buffalo transcended the imitative competitiveness that
characterizes so many campuses on the make and achieved an
excellence that was all its own.

Recently I spent a long weekend with several members of
the Buffalo group, many of whom are now in diaspora at other
universities. (Interestingly, several are acting university presidents
or are currently considering offers of college presidencies.) The talk
turned, as it inevitably does, to how thoroughly the Meyersonian
spirit has been stamped out at UB. "What went wrong?" someone
always asks.

The lion's share of the blame—or the credit, as some people
view it—goes to the current university administration. This admin-

istration simply denies history. Philosophically the Ketter administration is the successor of the Furnas administration. Meyerson's was the reign of an educational anti-Pope. There is rarely official mention of him or his works. For example, last year the American Council on Education released its current evaluation of the nation's graduate programs. Buffalo improved dramatically in the ACE ratings since the last survey was released, so much so that the jump was cited in the national press. The university proudly held a news conference at which campus officials announced that the upgrading of graduate education at Buffalo was largely accomplished under the late President Furnas. Meyerson had officially disappeared.

What saddens me is a suspicion that this gross assault would not be successful if we had been more effective. The stated goal of the Meyerson academic reorganization was to *transform* the university. How could a new administration turn her back so quickly if progress toward that goal had not been largely illusory or rhetorical? This is not a confession of failure. Nothing is so hard to change as a university, and Meyerson's attempt was courageous. But as one who was involved in many of the crucial decisions, I now see with all the unsettling clarity of hindsight that we undermined many of our own best aspirations for the university. If I were asked today how to bring about change in a university setting, I would offer the following guidelines:

(1) *Recruit with scrupulous honesty.* My personal recruiting at Buffalo depended on a falsely bright picture of the situation. It wasn't that I lied. But, consciously or not, I sweetened the package even when I was trying to be balanced and fair. Recruiting is a courtship ritual. The suitor displays his assets; the recruit, flattered by the attention and the promises, does not examine the assets closely. We were naive. The recruiting pitch at Buffalo depended on the future. We made little of the past and tended to deemphasize the present. Buffalo was the university of the future—of course, it would take time to catch up.

New arrivals had barely enrolled their kids in local schools before reality intruded. A labor-union dispute delayed construction of the promised new facilities. Inflation nibbled away at the buying power of the allocated construction funds at a rate of $1\frac{1}{2}$ per cent a month. It was easy to put up with the inconvenience of overcrowding when one was sure that the condition was temporary. But the dispute dragged on for months, and there was little room on the old campus. The situation might have been challenging if we had not led the new faculty to expect something magical. We had urged them to reveal their most creative, most imaginative educational thinking, then had assured them that their plans would receive generous support. In reality, money to staff new programs was difficult to come by. After one year, the state legislature began to pare the budget. Many new faculty members felt they had been conned. As recruiters we had not pointed out our ultimate inability to control the legislatively determined budget. We had promised a new university when our funds could provide only an architect's model.

Inadvertently, we had cooked up the classic recipe for revolution as suggested by Aaron Wildavsky: "Promise a lot; deliver a little. Teach people to believe that they will be much better off, but let there be no dramatic improvement. Try a variety of small programs but marginal in impact and severely under-financed. Avoid any attempted solution remotely comparable in size to the dimensions of the problem you are trying to solve."[2]

The intensity of the disaffection felt by some of those I had brought to the university came to me as a shock. We had raised expectations as high as any in modern educational history. When our program met only a part of these expectations, the disillusionment that followed was predictable and widespread. The disparity between vision and reality became intolerable. No one had said a word during the seductive recruiting days about triplicate forms, resentful colleagues, and unheeded requests for help from administrative headquarters.

Those who rose above the mundane annoyances provoked by university bureaucracy felt cheated in other ways. Recruits had joined our academic revolution because they shared our goal and wanted to participate. To keep such a cadre committed, an administration must keep them involved. But the warmth of our man-to-man recruiting interviews was not evident in later meetings with administrators. In fact, such meetings became fairly infrequent.

[2] "The Empty-Headed Blues: Black Rebellion and White Reaction," *The Public Interest*, Spring 1968, pp. 3–16.

The continuing evidence of personal support that might have overcome the unavoidable lack of concrete support was not forthcoming.

(2) *Guard against the Crazies.* Innovation is seductive. It
attracts interesting people. It also attracts people who will take your
ideas and distort them into something monstrous. You will then be
identified with the monster and will have to devote precious energy
to combatting it. A change-oriented administrator should be damned
sure about the persons he recruits, the persons who will be identified
as his men and women. A few of the persons who got administrative
posts under the new administration, committed though they were
to change, were so irresponsible or antagonistic that they alienated
more persons than they converted.

It is difficult to distinguish between agents of responsible
change and those who rend all they touch. The most successful
innovators often are marginal to the institution, almost in a geo-
graphical sense. They have contacts in other institutions, other areas.
Their credentials are unorthodox. They are often terrible company
men with little or no institutional loyalty. Change-oriented administrators must be able to distinguish the innovators, however eccen-
tric they may be, from the crazies. An academic community can
tolerate a high degree of eccentricity. But it will brutally reject an
individual it suspects of masking mediocrity with a flashy commitment to innovation.

(3) *Build support among like-minded people, whether or
not you recruited them.* Change-oriented administrators are particularly prone to act as though the organization came into being the
day they arrived. This is an illusion, an omnipotent fantasy. There
are no clean slates in established organizations. A new president
can't play Noah and build the world anew with two hand-picked
delegates from each academic discipline. Rhetoric about new starts
is frightening to those who suspect that the new beginning is the
end of their own careers. There can be no change without history,
without continuity.

What I think most of us in institutions want—and what
status, money, and power serve as currency for—is acceptance,
affection, and esteem. Institutions are more amenable to change
when they preserve the esteem of all members. Given economic
sufficiency, persons stay in organizations and feel satisfied in them

because they are respected and feel competent. They are much freer to identify with the adaptive process and much better equipped to tolerate the high level of ambiguity that accompanies change when these needs are heeded. Unfortunately, we did not attend to these needs at Buffalo.

The academic code, not the administrative one, determines appropriate behavior in the university. The president is a colleague, and he is expected to acknowledge his intellectual equals whatever their relative position on the administrative chart. Many old-guard professors took the administration's neglect as a personal snub. They were not asked for advice; they were not invited to social affairs. They suspected that we acted coolly toward them because we considered them to be second-rate academics who lacked intellectual chic and who could not cut it in Cambridge or New York.

Ironically, some of the old-guard academic administrators who kept their positions were notoriously second-rate. Meyerson extended the appointments of several such, perhaps hoping to avoid the appearance of a purge. Among the incumbents were a couple whose educational philosophy had rigidified sometime in the early fifties. Instead of appeasing the old guard, these appointments added insult. The old guard suspected that the new administration viewed them as an undifferentiated mass. They wondered why we kept these second-raters and overlooked a pool of potentially fine veteran candidates.

We succeeded in infusing new blood into Buffalo, but we failed to recirculate the old blood. We lost an opportunity to build loyalty among respected members of the veteran faculty. If veteran faculty members had been made to feel that they too had a future in the transformed university, they might have embraced the academic reorganization plan with some enthusiasm. Instead they were hurt, indignant, and—finally—angry.

(4) *Plan for how to change as well as what to change.* Buffalo had a plan for change, but we lacked a clear concept of how change should proceed. A statement of goals is not a program.

The Buffalo reorganization lacked the coherence and forcefulness that would have guaranteed its success. The fault may have been that it was too abstract. Or perhaps it was too much a pastiche. A great many influences were evident: Paul Goodman and the

community of colleges; the colleges and sense of academic tradition
of Oxbridge; the unorthodoxy and informality of Black Mountain;
the blurring of vocational-professional lives practiced at Antioch
and Bennington; the collegiality of Santa Cruz; the college-master
system of Yale. Each of these elements was both desirable and
educationally fashionable, but the mix never jelled. No alchemy
transformed the disparate parts into a living organism.

We had no coherent mechanisms for change. Instead we
relied on several partially realized administrative models. The burden of change fell upon the Faculty Senate, which emphasized the
small-group model. Change depended on three things: participation
by the persons involved, trust in the persons who advocated the
change, and clarity about the change itself. None of these conditions
was fully present at Buffalo, and, as a result, the change was im-
perfectly realized.

Radical students utilized a revolutionary model. The students
saw an opportunity for radical educational change in the Romantic
tradition. The administration relied heavily on the model of suc-
cessive limited comparisons, popularly known as "muddling
through." This is the model of most organizational decision-making.
It is a noncomprehensive, nontheoretical approach. Most administrators are forced to muddle through because the decisions they are
called upon to make are simply too complex to treat comprehen-
sively—even by committees. As a result, we neglected possible out-
comes, overlooked alternative solutions, and could not predict the
ultimate impact of the resulting policy on values.

Ultimately the reorganization failed to concentrate its energies on the model that would have satisfied the ambitions of all
parts of the university: an incremental-reform model. Revolution
inevitably produces reaction. All power to the French people one
day and to Thermidor the next. If change is to be permanent it
must be gradual. The incremental-reform model depends on a
rotating nucleus of persons who continuously read the data provided
by the organization and the society around it for clues that it is time
to adapt. These persons are not faddists but they are hypersensitive
to an idea whose hour has come. In a university such persons know
when an idea is antithetical to the values of an academic institution

and when it extends the definition of a university and makes it viable. One cannot structure these critical nuclei, but an organization cannot guarantee continuous self-renewal without them. At Buffalo a few departments and programs developed these nuclei. Most did not.

(5) *Don't settle for rhetorical change.* We accomplished the change at Buffalo by fiat. The Faculty Senate announced that the president's plan had been ratified.[3] Significant change does not take place that way. An organization has two structures: one on paper and another deep one that is a complex set of intramural relationships. A good administrator creates a good fit between the two. We allowed ourselves to be swept along by our rhetoric and neglected the much more demanding business of building new constituencies and maintaining established ones.

(6) *Don't allow those who are opposed to change to appropriate such basic issues as academic standards.* I became Meyerson's academic vice president in August 1968. Members of the old guard soon began to accuse me of being soft on standards. I had refused to disavow some of the more flagrant abuses of self-evaluation in the new colleges, and I had failed publicly to chastise faculty who subverted traditional academic practices as part of the radical revolution, although I did so unofficially. The problem of academic standards soon became a political issue. Privately we avowed our commitment to standards; publicly we were silent. The approach was notably unsuccessful. We did not want to undermine the fledgling colleges or violate the rights of radical faculty members. After Fascist, McCarthyite is the dirtiest word you can use on a liberal campus, and none of us was eager to hear it. We allowed the least change-oriented faculty members to make the issue of standards their own. They persuaded a great majority of moderate faculty members that the administration was committed to change for change's sake, whatever the price in academic excellence. We made a mistake that no successful reformer should ever make: we did not

[3] This was a good beginning but only that. Ratification occurred only two months after Meyerson arrived and almost a year before the plan was implemented. The senate that ratified the plan was not truly representative, and the plan itself was barely understood. Basically it was a "paper plan" with virtually no commitment except to a vague and poetic vision.

make sure that respectable people were unafraid of what was about
to happen.

(7) *Know the territory.* A peculiar balance exists between
the city of Buffalo and its one major university. Buffalo is not a
university town like Princeton or Ann Arbor. The university is not
powerful enough to impose its style and values on the city. Philadelphia and Los Angeles have several powerful universities that
divide attention and diffuse rancor. Buffalo has a single target for
its noisy antiintellectuals. Two years ago some powerful forces in
the town tried to close the university down. I don't know of another
campus in the country that has had to function with such constant
unsympathetic pressure from the surrounding community.[4] Meyerson barely had arrived in Buffalo when a group called Mothers
Against Meyerson (MAM) began to petition for his removal. Their
argument was that he was a Jew (a charge erroneously made
against Meyerson's predecessor by an earlier group, Mothers Against
Furnas) and that the campus harbored such dangerous criminal
types as critic Leslie Fiedler.

Buffalo blamed the disruptions of 1970 on the "permissive-
ness" of the new administration. I got mail recommending that
Curtis LeMay succeed Meyerson as university president. The local
exmarine who nominated LeMay believed that only the general's
exotic blend of authoritarianism and right-wing values could undo
the harm that we had perpetrated.

We never mastered the politics of local chauvinism. At the
same time that the national press was romancing the university,
one of the two local dailies was libeling her unmercifully. We
devoted too little energy and imagination to public relations at the
local level.

(8) *Appreciate environmental factors.* Like any other human activity, change proceeds more smoothly under optimal environmental conditions. Buffalo's chief environmental problem was
not its miserable weather. The problem at Buffalo was (and still is)

[4] This was true of university-community relations in 1970. From all I
have heard about Ketter's administration, the current UB president has
worked hard and successfully at reviving sympathy and support for the university among the Buffalo community.

overcrowding. The faculty we recruited expected to move their books into futuristic offices like those promised by the architect's model of the new campus. Instead, they moved in on top of the faculty already there. The university assembled some prefab annexes for the overflow. Barbara Solomon, writing on the paranoia at Buffalo, noted that we pursued the life of the mind in quarters so ugly as to seem calculated.

The new campus barely had begun to rise by the time we reached the originally proposed completion date of 1972. The university had to lease an interim campus near the new campus site. Eleven academic departments moved out to this temporary facility in the spring 1967. The leased buildings had been designed for commercial and light-industry use. The fifteen-minute bus trip was a drag for students, and the isolation of the interim campus was contrary to the whole spirit of the Meyerson plan.

We neglected to protect new programs from external forces. College A began an experimental program in community action that was housed off-campus because of space priorities. College A is located directly across from a parochial grammar school and a diocesan center for retarded children. Every time a Scarsdale Maoist wrote "F – – –" on the wall or a braless coed played her guitar in front of one of the stores residents of the neighborhood predictably reacted. Students of College A were determined to interact with their neighbors; mothers of the school children were equally determined not to interact. The mothers picketed. The whole business snow-balled, increasing the community's normally high level of outrage against the university.

(9) *Avoid future shock*. Buffalo aspired to be The University of the Year 2000. The future limited the campus just as the past limits the neurotic. The future insinuated itself into every attempt to deal with current issues and distorted our perception of the present. The unfinished new campus became an albatross, reminding everyone of the limited progress that was being made toward limitless goals. We put so much stock in the vision of future greatness that our disillusionment was inevitable. The problem with planning for the future is that there are no objective criteria against which to measure alternative solutions. There is not yet a contemporary

reality against which to test. As a result the planner generates future shlock along with valid ideas, and there's no sure-fire way to separate the two.

(10) *Allow time to consolidate gains.* The average tenure of a university president is now 4.4 years and decreasing. It is impossible to transform a university in so short a time. Only a year after Meyerson assumed the Buffalo presidency, rumors began to circulate that he was leaving. Supporters of the new administration feared abandonment. Social critic David Bazelon commented to me, "In every other university I've been to, the faculty hated the administration. Here they worry about desertion." The changes proposed by Meyerson depended on continued presidential support for their success. The campus had, in effect, undergone major surgery and did not have sufficient time to heal before a series of altogether different demands, including a semester of unrest, a new president, and a major recession, were made on it. When Meyerson finally did resign in late January 1970, it was as though someone had prematurely pulled out the stitches.

The last guideline I offer to the would-be university reformer is so basic that it might well come first:

(11) *Remember that change is most successful when those who are affected are involved in the planning.* This is a platitude of planning theory, and it is as true as it is trite. Nothing makes persons as resistant to new ideas or approaches as the feeling that change is being imposed upon them. The members of a university are unusually sensitive to individual prerogatives and to the administration's utter dependence on their support. Buffalo's academic plan was not popularly generated. Students and faculty did not contribute to its formulation. People resist change, even of a kind they basically agree with, if they are not significantly involved in the planning. A clumsier, slower, but more egalitarian approach to changing the university would have resulted in more permanent reform.

The problems surrounding innovation and change in an entrenched bureaucracy are not peculiar to universities. Every modern bureaucracy—university, government, or corporation—is essentially alike and responds similarly to challenge and to crisis.

Bureaucracy is the inevitable—and therefore necessary—

form for governing large and complex organizations. Essentially, we must find bureaucratic means to stimulate the pursuit of truth— the true nature of the organization's problems—in a spirit of free inquiry and with democratic methods. This search calls for those virtues our universities and colleges have proved so capable of inspiring in others: an examined life, a spirit of inquiry and genuine experimentation, a life based on discovering new realities, of taking risks, of suffering occasional defeats, and of not fearing the surprise of the future.

The model for truly innovative and creative organizations in an era of enormous change becomes nothing less than the scientific spirit. The model for science becomes the model for all.

Index

Term appointment for president, 23, 82–83

Theory vs. practice, 4, 12

TOLLEY, W., 19

TOUSTER, S., 95, 114, 115, 122; as promoter of Buffalo, 112–113; questioning of Bennis by, 116–117; as recruiter, 121

TRILLING, L., 7

Trustees/directors, boards of: as aid to president, 83–84; characteristics of, 85; and Cincinnati search, 67–68; as community buffers, 84; at Northwestern, 22; selecting, 84; and Stanford search, 59; at SUNY, 40, 52, 55, 60–63

TUNNEY, J., 74

U

University: as bureaucracy, 2, 5, 11–12; change in, 136–145; as community of scholars, 72; crisis in, 12, 27; defense research by, 71; as democratic community, 64; esteem in, 139; exoteric knowledge about, 5; finance problems of, 76; inner workings of, 1; metaphors for, 77–79; morality in, 13; paranoia in, 2; political intervention and presidential succession in, 58; public understanding of, 2; training administrators for, 81. *See also* Organizations; President; Search

V

VON MOLTKE, K., 92, 94

W

WADDINGTON, C. H., 131

WALLACE, H., 102

WEAVER, J. C., 52

WELCH, C., 53, 91

WELLS, H. B., 17

WESTMORELAND, W., 52

WHITE, A. S., 19

WICKER, T., 9, 13, 14

WILDAVSKY, A., 137

WILLENBROCK, K., 116, 122, 130, 131

WITHERSPOON, G., 79

WOLFE, T., 8

WRIGHT, F. L., houses of, 122–123, 131

Y

YEVTUSHENKO, Y., 15

Z

Z, 53

ZWEIG, F., 126